TAX EFFORT AND TAX POTENTIAL IN TIMOR-LESTE

ASSESSING POST-PANDEMIC FISCAL CHALLENGES AND PRIORITIES

JULY 2024

ADB

ASIAN DEVELOPMENT BANK

© 2024 Asian Development Bank
6 ADB Avenue, Mandaluyong City, 1550 Metro Manila, Philippines
Tel +63 2 8632 4444; Fax +63 2 8636 2444
www.adb.org

Some rights reserved. Published in 2024.

ISBN 978-92-9270-737-8 (print), 978-92-9270-738-5 (PDF); 978-92-9270-739-2 (ebook)
Publication Stock No. SPR240293-2
DOI: http://dx.doi.org/10.22617/SPR240293-2

Notes:
This study was prepared under TA 9122-TIM: Timor-Leste, Fiscal Policy for Improved Service Delivery by Joao Tovar Jalles, Lisbon School of Economics and Management (ISEG), University of Lisbon.
The report does not necessarily reflect the views of the author's affiliated institutions, ADB or the Government concerned.
In this publication, "$" refers to United States dollars.

On the cover: Illustration 125341019 © Melpomenem | Dreamstime.com.

CONTENTS

TABLES, FIGURES, AND BOX

Tables

Figures

Box

FOREWORD

Economic diversification is essential for the growth and development in Timor-Leste. With petroleum revenues declining, fiscal reforms are also needed to improve service delivery and sustain the country's sovereign wealth fund. There is potential for improved domestic revenue collection and rationalization of public expenditure.

The Asian Development Bank (ADB) has provided support to the government in building capacity to design and implement reforms. Since 2015, when the Government of Timor-Leste's Fiscal Reform Commission was established, ADB has also provided technical assistance to support the development of regulatory frameworks around the establishment of state-owned enterprises and autonomous public agencies for public service delivery.

This study is very timely as it provides a background to Timor-Leste's tax system and strengthens the understanding of the country's tax effort and long-run tax buoyancy, suggesting that growth has improved fiscal sustainability over time. The study builds government capacity for evidence-based fiscal policy. Consultations with government stakeholders have identified the strengthening of tax policy and legal frameworks as a critical step to improving domestic resource mobilization and revenue collection. The findings of the study are closely aligned with Timor-Leste's strategic economic development direction and with ADB's country partnership strategy for the country.

I would like to express my sincere appreciation for Director General Jose Alexandre de Carvalho, Planning and Budgeting Division, Ministry of Finance, for identifying this important area of work. Along with Director Epifanio Martins and colleagues at the Ministry of Finance, he has provided important policy guidance and statistical support to the study. I thank ADB for the expertise provided through Professor João Tovar Jalles for this work and the continued knowledge support to Timor-Leste.

Helder Lopes
Governor, Banco Central de Timor-Leste

PREFACE

Domestic resource mobilization (DRM) is a critical aspect of a country's economic development and sustainable growth. A government's ability to raise funds and resources from within its own borders determines its capacity to finance various public services, infrastructure projects, and social programs. DRM encompasses a wide range of revenue generation strategies, including taxation, natural resource utilization, foreign direct investment, and more. At a time when fiscal policy plays a crucial role in most countries' economic recovery efforts, understanding and effectively implementing DRM strategies is essential for a nation's fiscal health, and its ability to meet the needs and aspirations of its citizens.

Tax revenue plays a central and substantial role in DRM and is often the largest single source of revenue for governments. Income taxes, corporate taxes, value-added taxes, and other forms of taxation contribute significantly to a country's budget. Tax revenue and economic growth have a complex and interdependent relationship which can vary based on tax policies, economic conditions, and the overall tax system of a country.

Timor-Leste and several other Southeast Asian countries have experienced fluctuations in revenue due to their dependence on a narrow range of commodities. A diversified DRM approach can provide stability in government finances by reducing vulnerability to global market fluctuations.

The Asian Development Bank (ADB) recognizes the important contribution of a sound tax policy and efficient tax administration system toward ensuring effective DRM in the Asia and Pacific region. ADB has initiated various program measures aimed at improving developing member countries' DRM efforts through policy advice and institutional capacity building.

It is a privilege for ADB to support this study, which provides Timor-Leste with valuable insights on the context of its tax potential, the level of tax effort, and the measure of tax buoyancy as the government assesses the growth elasticity and flexibility of the existing tax system. We hope this study will substantiate DRM policy reforms for Timor-Leste, and open other areas for collaboration with the government.

On behalf of ADB, I would like to express my appreciation for the excellent cooperation with the Government of Timor-Leste in preparing this report.

Winfried Wicklein
Director General
Southeast Asia Department
Asian Development Bank

ABBREVIATIONS

CF	Christiano–Fitzgerald
CIT	corporate income tax
COVID-19	coronavirus disease
DRM	domestic revenue/resource mobilization
FCAS	Fragile and conflict-affected situations
GDP	gross domestic product
HP	Hodrick-Prescott
IMF	International Monetary Fund
LIC	low-income country
PIT	personal income tax
SDG	Sustainable Development Goal
VAT	value-added tax

I RECENT ECONOMIC DEVELOPMENTS

A. Regional

Fragile and conflict-affected situations (FCAS)[1] such as Timor-Leste typically experience higher aggregate economic volatility and worse macroeconomic performance than other countries.[2] Conflict usually affects a country's rate of growth following the negative impacts on the stocks of both physical and human capital as well as disrupted markets and reduced trust. These effects are long-lasting and Timor-Leste is no exception, given the decades of conflict and violence experienced during Indonesian occupation before independence in 2002.[3] Figure 1 plots the interquartile range of real gross domestic product (GDP) growth in FCAS and advanced economies with the former group being characterized by heightened heterogeneity.

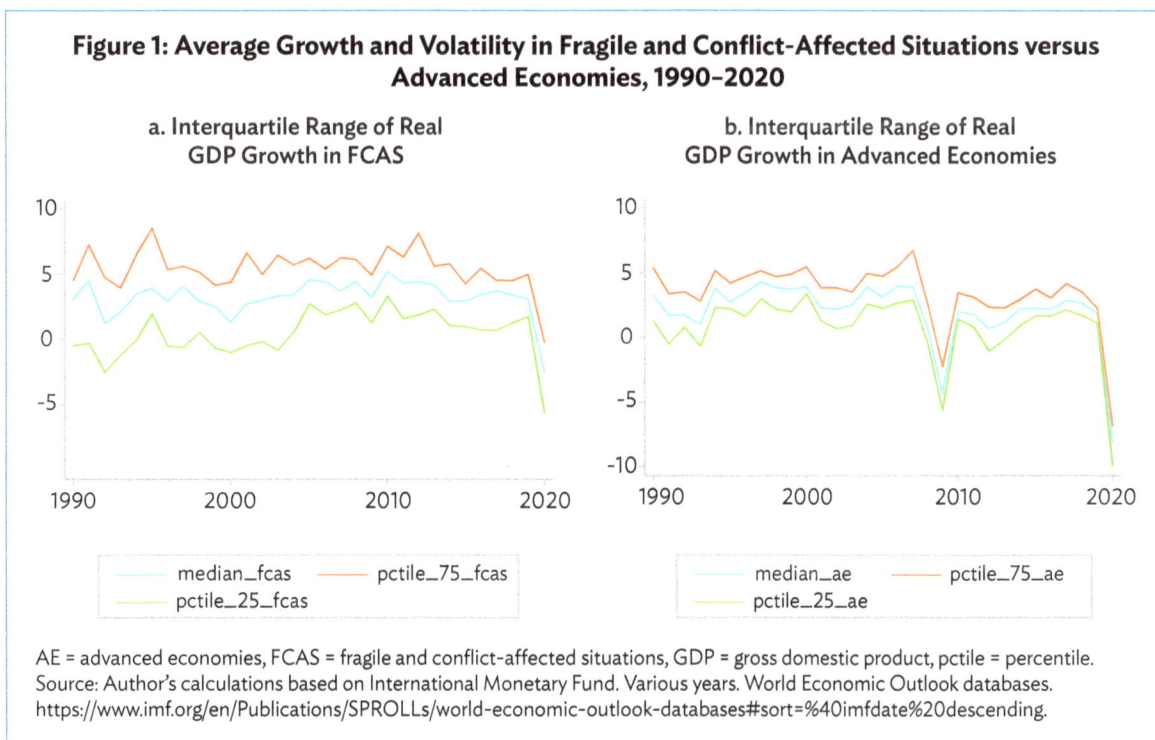

Figure 1: Average Growth and Volatility in Fragile and Conflict-Affected Situations versus Advanced Economies, 1990–2020

a. Interquartile Range of Real GDP Growth in FCAS

b. Interquartile Range of Real GDP Growth in Advanced Economies

AE = advanced economies, FCAS = fragile and conflict-affected situations, GDP = gross domestic product, pctile = percentile.
Source: Author's calculations based on International Monetary Fund. Various years. World Economic Outlook databases. https://www.imf.org/en/Publications/SPROLLs/world-economic-outlook-databases#sort=%40imfdate%20descending.

---

1   A country is considered FCAS if the average rating is 3.2 or less in the country performance assessment of the Asian Development Bank (ADB) and the World Bank's country policy and institutional assessment. The average score for Timor-Leste is 3.1 | Independent Evaluation Department. 2021. Timor-Leste: Validation of the Country Partnership Strategy Final Review, 2016–2020. Manila: ADB. https://www.adb.org/sites/default/files/evaluation-document/678771/files/cpsfrv-tim-2016-2020.pdf.

2   There is considerable literature on the causes of macroeconomic volatility. See W. Easterly, R. Islam, and J.E. Stiglitz. 2001. Shaken and Stirred: Explaining Growth Volatility. In B. Pleskovic and N. Stern, eds. *Annual World Bank Conference on Development Economics 2000.* pp. 191–211. Washington, DC: The World Bank. https://openknowledge.worldbank.org/handle/10986/14010. | T. Beck et al. 2001. Financial Structure and Economic Development: Firm, Industry, and Country Evidence. In A. Demirgüç-Kunt and R. Levine, eds. *Financial Structure and Economic Growth: A Cross-Country Comparison of Banks, Markets, and Development.* pp. 189–242. The MIT Press. | N.V. Loayza et al. 2007. Macroeconomic Volatility and welfare in developing countries: an introduction. *World Bank Economic Review.* 21 (3). pp. 343-357. Washington, DC: World Bank Group. September. http://documents.worldbank.org/curated/en/577091468180899931/Macroeconomic-volatility-and-welfare-in-developing-countries-an-introduction.

3   GDP per capita growth during conflict was strongly negative as seen in Azerbaijan, Croatia, Georgia, Guinea-Bissau, Liberia, Nicaragua, Rwanda, Sierra Leone, Solomon Islands, and Tajikistan. | J.F.E. Ohiorhenuan. 2011. The future of poverty and development in Africa. *Foresight.* 13 (3). pp. 7–23. Emerald Group Publishing Limited. https://doi.org/10.1108/14636681111138730.

In face of uncertain times going forward (Figure 2), ultimately, building economic and fiscal resilience in Timor-Leste should be central to post-pandemic recovery as well as preparedness for the future. There are multiple definitions for resilience, but according to the United States Economic Development Administration, economic resilience refers to "the ability to withstand, prevent or quickly recover from major disruptions—or shocks—to its underlying economic base".[4] Building resilience requires a solid understanding of economic opportunities and challenges, and it is country-specific. Timor-Leste must prioritize strengthening of fiscal resilience, specifically by focusing on domestic revenue (or resource) mobilization (DRM) strategies.

Figure 2: World Uncertainty Index from Quarter 1, 1990 to Quarter 1, 2021

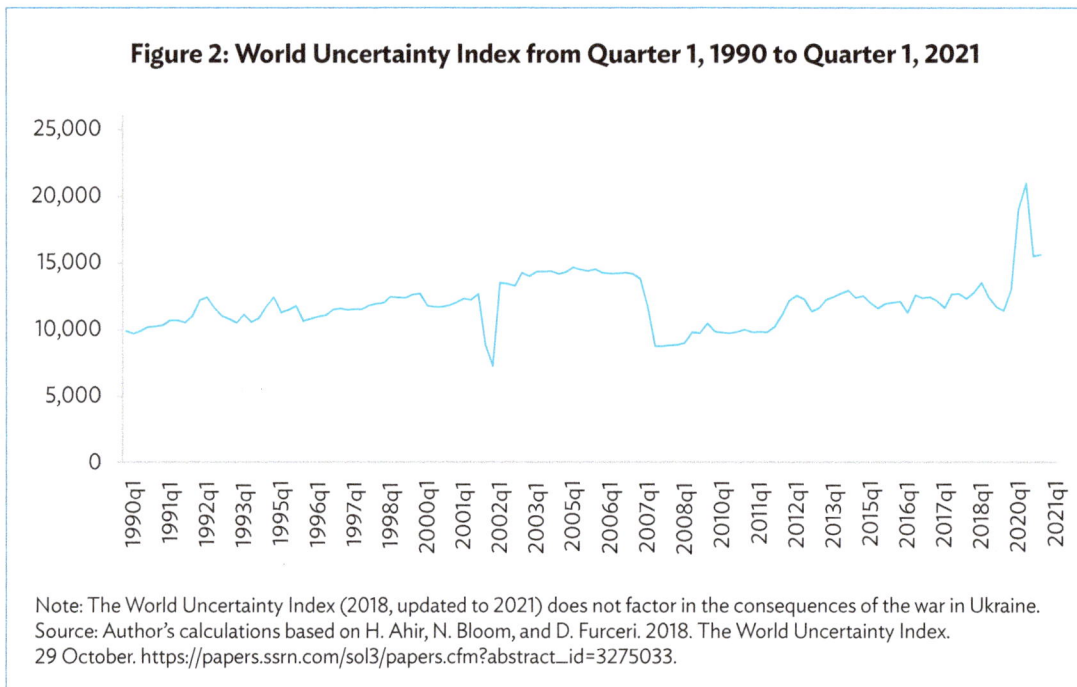

Note: The World Uncertainty Index (2018, updated to 2021) does not factor in the consequences of the war in Ukraine.
Source: Author's calculations based on H. Ahir, N. Bloom, and D. Furceri. 2018. The World Uncertainty Index. 29 October. https://papers.ssrn.com/sol3/papers.cfm?abstract_id=3275033.

B. Timor-Leste

Timor-Leste is a physically and economically small and vulnerable island-type developing country, heavily dependent on petroleum income for growth.[5] Since its independence in 2002, Timor-Leste has been facing challenges in rebuilding its infrastructure, strengthening the civil administration, and generating jobs for young people entering the workforce. The development of offshore oil and gas resources has greatly supplemented government revenues. This technology-intensive industry, however, has done little to create jobs partly because Timor-Leste possesses no production facilities. The country remains one of poorest in Southeast Asia, heavily dependent on foreign aid. Structurally, economic liberalization has stalled.

In macroeconomic terms, output fluctuations in Timor-Leste reflect its narrow economic base and heavy dependence on oil exports.[6] After reaching an all-time high year-on-year real growth in gross domestic product (GDP) of 11.3% in 2008, growth decelerated in 2009 and it has been below the two digits since 2010. In terms of production structure, 70% of the population depends on subsistence agriculture though the shares of primary activities in GDP have been declining over time (due to declining fish catches). In contrast, the shares of construction and services (mainly transport, communications, and government administration) have been increasing.[7]

---

4   Vulnerability to shocks is a big obstacle to economic progress resulting in lower and more volatile growth. | International Monetary Fund. 2011. Managing Volatility: A Vulnerability Exercise for Low-Income Countries. *IMF Policy Papers*. Washington, DC. 10 March. https://www.imf.org/en/Publications/Policy-Papers/Issues/2016/12/31/Managing-Volatility-A-Vulnerability-Exercise-for-Low-Income-Countries-PP4540.
5   Timor-Leste is one of eight ADB member countries identified as being both FCAS and a small island developing state (SIDS).
6   The narrow asset base consists of resource extraction, agriculture and tourism, all of which are highly vulnerable to market shocks. In addition, Timor-Leste is also vulnerable to natural disaster-related shocks.
7   International Monetary Fund. 2021. Timor-Leste: 2021 Article IV Consultation-Press Release; Staff Report; and Statement by the

Following the coronavirus disease (COVID-19) pandemic, in 2020, real GDP growth of Timor-Leste dipped to −7.6% but it is expected to recover to 1.8% in 2022 (Figure 3, panel a). Inflation has averaged 5% yearly since 2002 with big fluctuations (from −11% in 2004 to +24% in 2019) owing to oil price volatility (Figure 3, panel b). While the pandemic

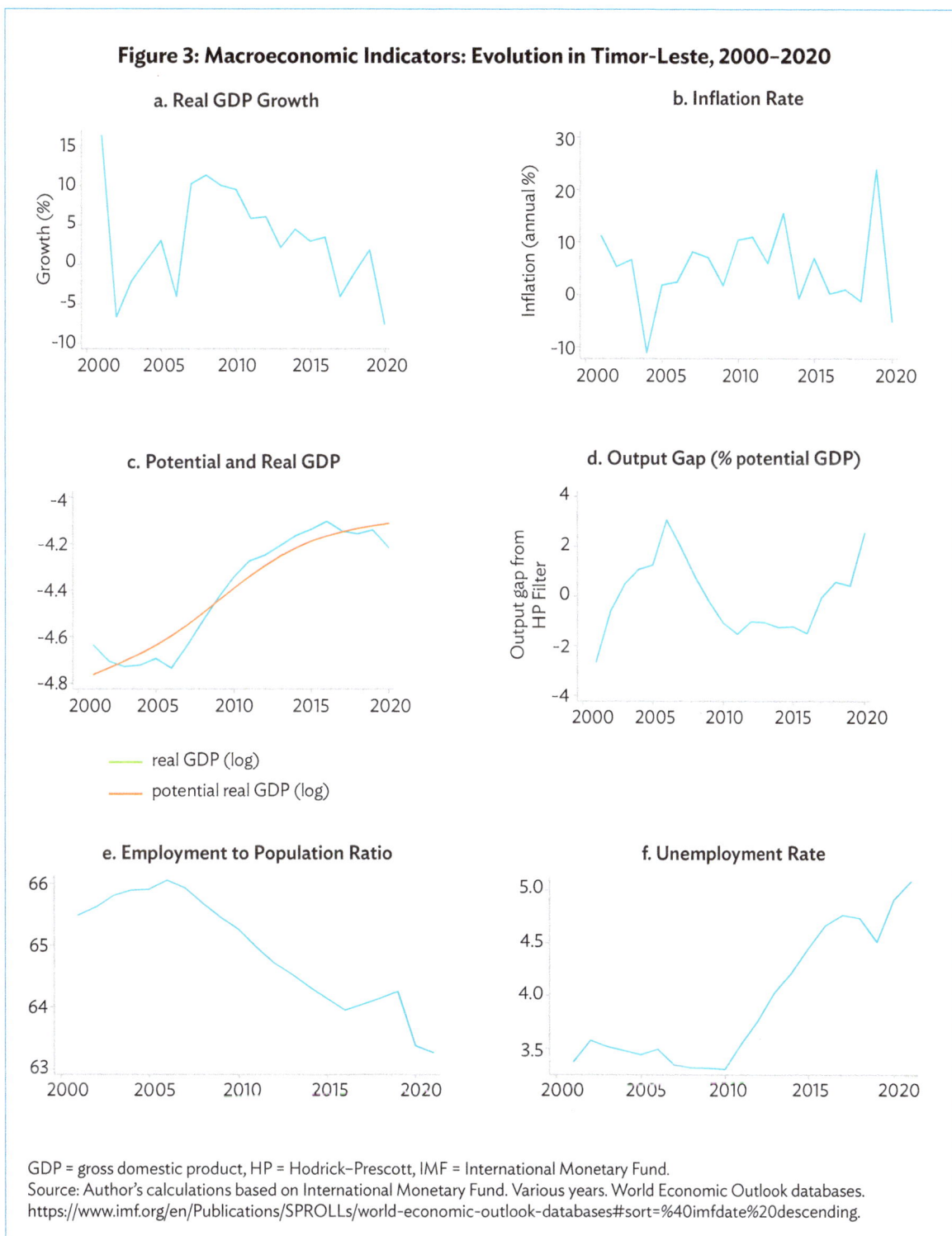

Figure 3: Macroeconomic Indicators: Evolution in Timor-Leste, 2000–2020

a. Real GDP Growth

b. Inflation Rate

c. Potential and Real GDP

— real GDP (log)
— potential real GDP (log)

d. Output Gap (% potential GDP)

e. Employment to Population Ratio

f. Unemployment Rate

GDP = gross domestic product, HP = Hodrick–Prescott, IMF = International Monetary Fund.
Source: Author's calculations based on International Monetary Fund. Various years. World Economic Outlook databases. https://www.imf.org/en/Publications/SPROLLs/world-economic-outlook-databases#sort=%40imfdate%20descending.

Executive Director for Timor-Leste. *IMF Staff Country Reports*. Country Report No. 2021/152. Washington, DC. 14 July. https://www.imf.org/en/Publications/CR/Issues/2021/07/14/Timor-Leste-2021-Article-IV-Consultation-Press-Release-Staff-Report-and-Statement-by-the-462155.

reinforced the deceleration in potential GDP growth, such downward trend started earlier (in 2011) suggesting that structural factors have been the major cause (flattening of the log curve in Figure 3, panel c). The pandemic shock caused the output gap to reach over 2.5% of potential GDP in 2020 (Figure 3, panel d).[8] Labor market variables were also negatively affected by the pandemic with employment–population ratio falling to close to 63% while the unemployment rose to more than 5% (Figure 3, panels e and f).

---

8   Refer to Appendix 1 for a more formal discussion on Timor-Leste's potential GDP–output gap over time including a discussion on recent practical approaches for their estimation.

A. Regional

The revenue performance of developing Asia as a region has improved since 2000. The average tax-to-gross domestic product (GDP) ratio increased from about 13% in 2000 to 17% in 2018, which is similar to the increase observed in Latin America and the Caribbean (LAC) countries (Figure 4). About one-half of the tax revenue increase came from rising value-added tax (VAT) collections (Figure 5). This is despite the fact that the typical standard VAT rate in developing Asia is lower than in other regions of the world (e.g., in 2020, the standard rate was 19% in advanced economies and 15% in LAC). The widespread adoption of a broad-based consumption tax, such as the VAT, by most developing Asia has strengthened tax administration as countries began relying on digital technologies in their tax system (e.g., electronic filing systems) which helped improve compliance.[9]

Figure 4: Tax Revenue for Selected Regions, 2000–2018

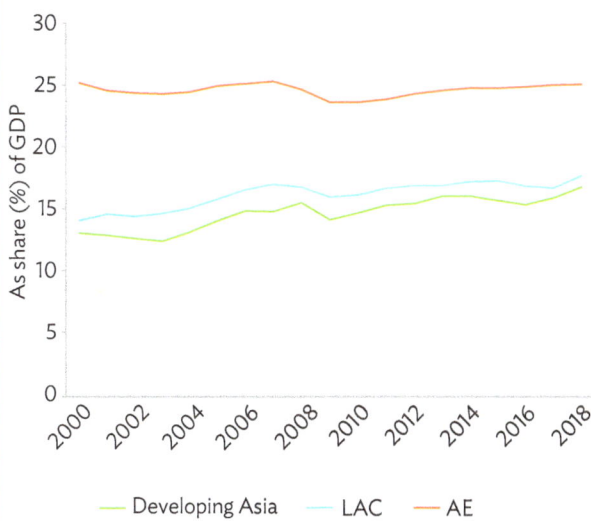

AE = advanced economies, GDP = gross domestic product, LAC = Latin America and the Caribbean.
Source: International Monetary Fund. Various years. World Economic Outlook databases. https://www.imf.org/en/Publications/SPROLLs/world-economic-outlook-databases#sort=%40imfdate%20descending.

Figure 5: Value-Added Tax Revenue for Selected Regions, 2000–2017

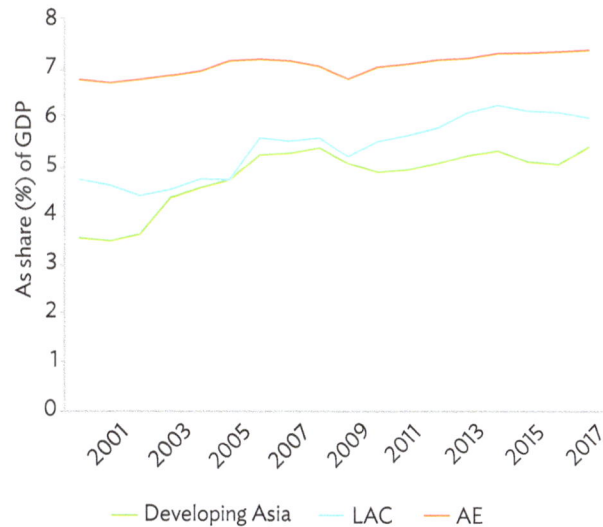

AE = advanced economies, GDP = gross domestic product, LAC = Latin America and the Caribbean.
Source: International Monetary Fund. Various years. World Economic Outlook databases. https://www.imf.org/en/Publications/SPROLLs/world-economic-outlook-databases#sort=%40imfdate%20descending.

9   S. Gupta and J. T. Jalles. 2022a. Tax Revenue Reforms and Income Distribution in Developing Countries. Economic Modelling. 110, 105804. ScienceDirect, Elsevier. May. https://www.sciencedirect.com/science/article/pii/S0264999322000505. | E-filing of tax returns has spread from developed to developing countries. This type of reform can reduce (i) errors and opportunities for corruption, and (ii) taxpayer compliance costs. | J. Coolidge and F. Yilmaz. 2014. Can specialized tax software reduce tax compliance costs in developing countries?. Investment Climate. World Bank Group. https://documents1.worldbank.org/curated/en/690221468152705219/pdf/907560BRI00Box0Tax0Compliance0Costs.pdf#:~:text=The%20World%20Bank%20Group%20conducted%20a%20study%2C%20using,software%20in%20attempting%20to%20optimize%20their%20tax%20liabilities.

The increase in VAT revenues was accompanied by stable receipts from trade taxes and higher receipts from excise taxes.[10] Economic literature considers high reliance on trade taxes as unfriendly to economic growth.[11] This outcome in developing Asia is contrary to trends observed in low-income countries (LICs), where trade revenues in relation to GDP, on average, have declined.[12] This result is surprising for a region heavily reliant on trade.[13] It is unclear whether this fact is attributable to the use of conventional tariffs or other charges. Revenues from excisable goods, such as tobacco, alcohol, motor vehicles, and fuel, increased by one-third, reflecting adoption of a sound policy to tax harmful externalities. Revenues from corporate income tax (CIT) also increased by about 1% of GDP, despite falling CIT rates and concerns with tax planning by multinational enterprises. The CIT revenues have held up despite falling CIT rates in developing Asia, which declined on average from 30% in 2000 to 22% in 2018.[14] The personal income tax (PIT) revenues increased by a percentage point of GDP, reflecting the growing ability of developing Asia to put more complex tax systems in place and to bring growing incomes in the formal sector into the tax net. Property taxes are in use in the region but do not yield much revenue. In the aggregate, the ratio of direct to indirect taxes has worsened

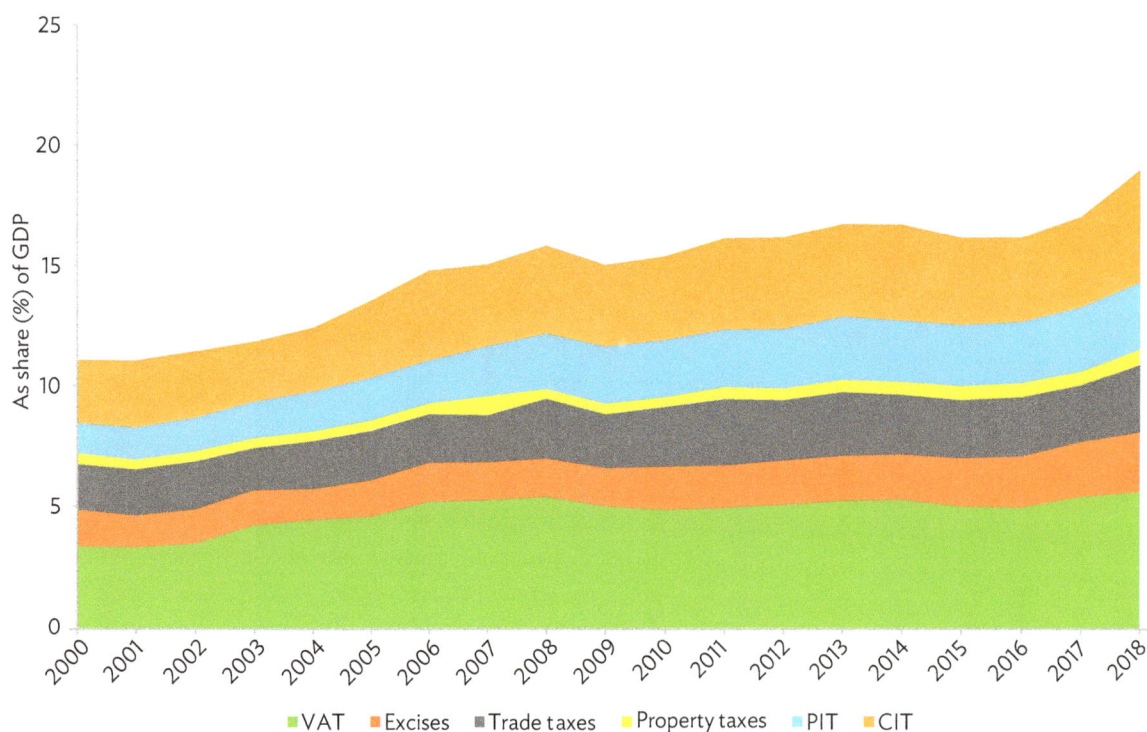

Figure 6: Tax Revenue by Type in Developing Asia, 2000–2018

CIT = corporate income tax, PIT = personal income tax, VAT = value-added tax.
Source: International Monetary Fund. Various years. World Economic Outlook databases. https://www.imf.org/en/Publications/SPROLLs/world-economic-outlook-databases#sort=%40imfdate%20descending.

---

10   Changes in tax components do not necessarily add up to cumulative increase in tax-to-GDP ratio because of varying sample sizes for different tax types.
11   For a detailed discussion on taxation and its relationship with long-term economic growth, see International Monetary Fund. 2015. Fiscal Policy and Long-term Growth. *IMF Policy Papers.* Washington, DC. 20 April. https://www.imf.org/en/Publications/Policy-Papers/Issues/2016/12/31/Fiscal-Policy-and-Long-Term-Growth-PP4964.
12   P. Mullins, S. Gupta, and J. Liu. 2020. Domestic Revenue Mobilization in Low-Income Countries: Where to from Here? Center for Global Development Policy Paper 195. Washington, DC: Center for Global Development. 10 December. https://www.cgdev.org/sites/default/files/PP195-Gupta-LICs-DRM.pdf.
13   For instance, over the past 30 years, trade openness—defined as exports plus imports over GDP—in developing Asia amounted to 93% in contrast with the 71% of LAC.
14   The decline in corporate tax rates coupled with robust corporate tax collection is a worldwide phenomenon.

over time, with revenue increases from indirect taxes larger than those from direct taxes (Figure 6). This suggests that the tax system has become more regressive over time.[15]

B. Timor-Leste

Most government revenue in Timor-Leste comes from offshore petroleum projects in the Timor Sea. More specifically, oil and gas account for more than 95% of government revenue or above 30% of GDP,[16] which is consigned to a Petroleum Fund.[17] However, the balance of the Petroleum Fund dropped by $1 billion in 2018 at the cost of large withdrawals and negative investment returns.[18] The Timorese economy depends largely on government expenditures funded by drawdowns from the Petroleum Fund. Government spending has amounted to about 80% of GDP over the past 3 years. About 85% of government expenditure is financed from the country's Petroleum Fund.[19] The largest component is public consumption (around 35% of GDP in 2019) followed by spending in capital formation and social protection (each amounting to 20% of GDP in 2019) (Figure 7). Domestic revenue declined in recent years from an already low base, despite a large increase in withholding tax collections. Domestic revenues are also low (reaching about 12% of non-oil GDP) in comparison with other fragile states such as Liberia, Malawi, or Nepal (around 15%–20% of GDP).[20] Tax revenues account for two-third of this (so 7.5% of non-oil GDP) and are also low in relative terms.

Domestic revenue mobilization could rely on a revised tax procedure code or the adoption of a VAT (section IV.B). In terms of composition, within taxes, taxes on income, profits, and capital gains take the largest share of total revenues (around 25% in 2019) followed by taxes on goods and services and international trade (together 5% in 2019) (Figure 7). The top individual income and corporate tax rates are 10%.

Consequently, the government deficit remains large (projected to reach 53.9% of non-oil GDP in 2022) and public debt has been on a worryingly rapid rising trend which increased from 2.8% in 2015 to close to 19% of non-oil GDP in 2022 (Figure 8).[21] Efforts toward DRM therefore remain important to secure medium-term fiscal sustainability, although delays in the implementation of important fiscal reforms due to political–economic aspects have been a key constraint.[22] That said, strong fiscal adjustments in the near term could hurt the population's living standards and affect the basic functioning of the Timorese government.

The COVID-19 pandemic in conjunction with Cyclone Seroja in April 2021 (leading to floods, landslides, human loss, and economic damage) had serious consequences for the economy of Timor-Leste.[23] Imports declined by 19%, particularly due to a slowdown in construction and travel services. Exports nearly halved, owing to limited travel services and lower coffee earnings. From a fiscal policy standpoint, following the pandemic-related shock, public expenditure dropped by 9%. Capital spending nearly halved, but public transfers increased to support households.[24] Domestic revenues suffered from lower economic activity, while the fiscal deficit eased to 17% of GDP in 2020, mostly due to lower spending.[25] In fact, fiscal policy in Timor-Leste has not been stabilizing macroeconomic fluctuations over

---

15   Footnote 9 (1st citation).
16   Footnote 1.
17   Established in 2005, the Petroleum Fund is to serve as a repository for all petroleum reserves and to preserve the value of Timor-Leste's future wealth. The IMF forecasts that this fund will shrink rapidly in the coming years. | Footnote 7.
18   World Bank Group. 2019. *Timor-Leste Economic Report, April 2019: Moving Beyond Uncertainty.* Washington, DC: World Bank. https://openknowledge.worldbank.org/handle/10986/31706.
19   A World Bank assessment showed that Petroleum Fund withdrawals financed most of public spending, but its revenues have declined sharply since 2012. See, World Bank. 2020. *Timor-Leste Economic Report: Towards a Sustainable Recovery.* Washington, DC: World Bank. https://openknowledge.worldbank.org/handle/10986/34748. | Footnote 1.
20   Footnote 7.
21   Public debt is exclusively composed of concessional lending. The most recent IMF Debt Sustainability Analysis (2022) classified Timor-Leste as a country of moderate risk of debt distress.
22   Merits of fiscal reforms and their impact are discussed later in the report.
23   World Bank Group. 2021. *Timor-Leste Economic Report: Charting a New Path.* Washington, DC: World Bank. https://openknowledge.worldbank.org/handle/10986/35720.
24   Footnote 23.
25   Footnote 23.

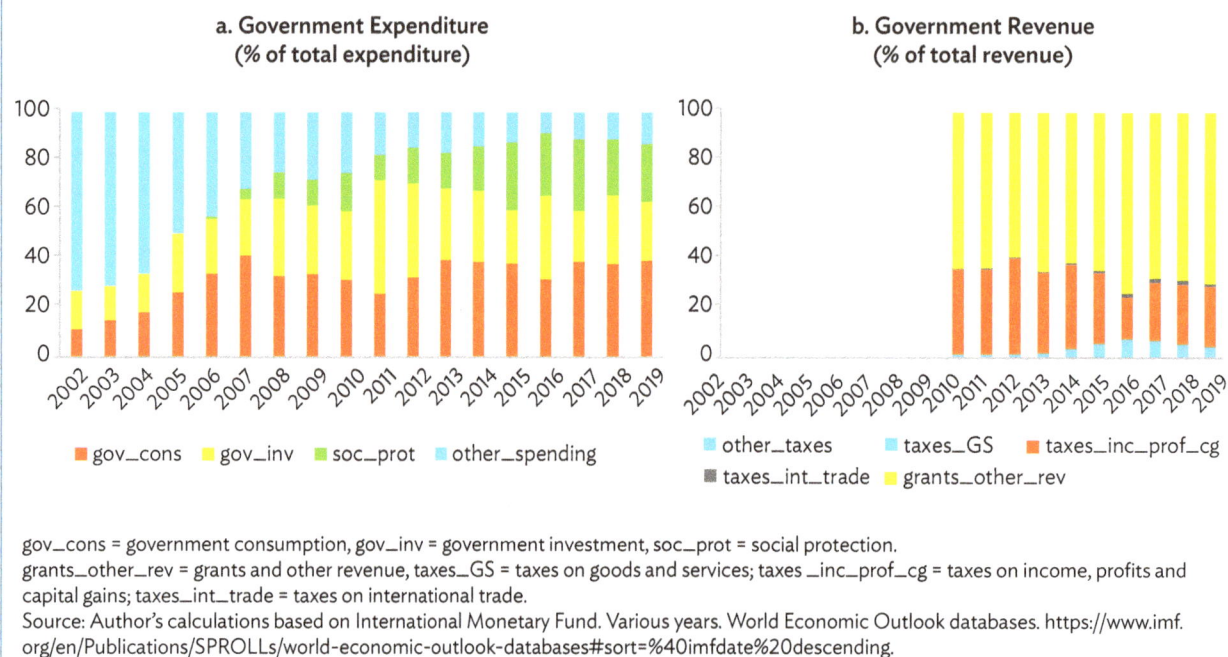

Figure 7: Decomposition of Expenditure and Revenue in Timor-Leste, 2002–2019

a. Government Expenditure
(% of total expenditure)

b. Government Revenue
(% of total revenue)

gov_cons = government consumption, gov_inv = government investment, soc_prot = social protection.
grants_other_rev = grants and other revenue, taxes_GS = taxes on goods and services; taxes_inc_prof_cg = taxes on income, profits and capital gains; taxes_int_trade = taxes on international trade.
Source: Author's calculations based on International Monetary Fund. Various years. World Economic Outlook databases. https://www.imf.org/en/Publications/SPROLLS/world-economic-outlook-databases#sort=%40imfdate%20descending.

the last couple of decades. Automatic stabilizers are absent and they need to be reinforced to increase resilience to future shocks.[26]

In sum, in Timor-Leste, the medium-term expected decline in the Petroleum Fund together with a chronically large budget deficit (Figure 8, panel a) calls for sharp fiscal adjustment. In this context, DRM is of paramount importance not just for fiscal sustainability but also for post-pandemic recovery and development (discussed in section III). Hence, an immediate challenge is to contain the fiscal deficit within the limits of available financing, in a manner consistent with the enhancement of the country's macroeconomic stability.

Challenges related to the political economy appear to complicate matters. Timor-Leste's economic freedom score is 46.3, putting it in the category of repressed, making its economy the 164th freest in the 2022 Index out of 177 countries.[27] Timor-Leste's low score is driven by weak property rights. It is ranked 38th among 40 countries in the Asia and Pacific region, and its overall economic freedom score is below the regional and world averages. The economy of Timor-Leste has registered few signs of freedom since its inclusion in the Index in 2009. Other impediments to greater economic freedom are corruption, which weakens government integrity and effectiveness of the judicial system.[28] Against this background, economic literature investigating the relationship between institutional conditions and economic performance suggests governance and institutional quality as important growth drivers.[29] Ultimately, strong

---

26 Refer to Appendix 2 for a technical discussion on overall degree of fiscal counter-cyclicality of Timor-Leste in particular and FCAS in general.
27 The Heritage Foundation. 2022. 2022 Index of Economic Freedom. Washington, DC.
28 The World Bank estimates that as much as 2% of GDP is lost annually to corruption. | As quoted in United Nations. 2019. The Anti-Corruption Commission in Timor-Leste builds its capacities to investigate corruption and financial crimes. 11 January. https://www.unodc.org/roseap/en/what-we-do/anti-corruption/topics/29-the-anti-corruption-commission-in-timor-leste-builds-its-capacities-to-investigate-corruption-and-financial-crimes.html#:~:text=Building%20on%20the%20World%20Bank,USD%20annually%20due%20to%20corruption.
29 For example, see J. Benhabib and A. Rustichini. 1996. Social conflict and growth. *Journal of Economic Growth*. 1. pp. 125–142. Springer Nature. March. https://doi.org/10.1007/BF00163345. | D. Acemoglu et al. 2003. Institutional causes, macroeconomic symptoms: volatility, crises and growth. Journal of Monetary Economics. 50 (1). pp. 49–123. ScienceDirect, Elsevier. January. https://www.sciencedirect.com/science/article/abs/pii/S0304393202002088. | J. Klomp and J. de Haan. 2009. Central bank independence and financial instability. *Journal of Financial Stability*. 5 (4). pp. 321-338. ScienceDirect, Elsevier. December. https://doi.org/10.1016/j.jfs.2008.10.001.

Figure 8: Evolution of Fiscal Aggregates in Timor-Leste, 2015–2022 (Projected)

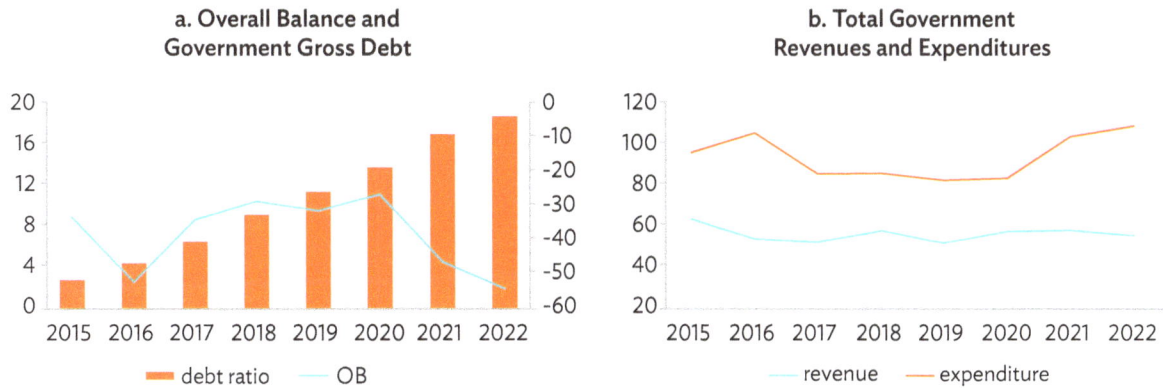

a. Overall Balance and Government Gross Debt

b. Total Government Revenues and Expenditures

Notes:
1. Debt ratio = public government gross debt as a percentage of non-oil gross domestic product (GDP) plotted on primary y-axis on the left.
2. OB = government overall budget balance as a percentage of non-oil GDP, plotted on secondary y-axis on the right.
3. Revenue and expenditure on panel b presented as a percentage of non-oil GDP.

Source: Author's calculations using IMF Article IV data. International Monetary Fund. 2021. Timor-Leste: 2021 Article IV Consultation-Press Release; Staff Report; and Statement by the Executive Director for Timor-Leste. *IMF Staff Country Reports.* No. 2021/152. Washington, DC. 14 July. https://www.imf.org/en/Publications/CR/Issues/2021/07/14/Timor-Leste-2021-Article-IV-Consultation-Press-Release-Staff-Report-and-Statement-by-the-462155.

and legitimate leaderships of the state are needed to foster and protect an enabling environment for economic activity that can promote security, growth, and inclusiveness in Timor-Leste.

III REVENUE MOBILIZATION STRATEGY IN TIMOR-LESTE

A. Domestic Revenue Mobilization for Inclusive Growth

Improving domestic revenue mobilization (DRM), especially among developing countries, has gained renewed attention over the past few years.[30] In fact, the Addis Agenda on financing for development pays particular attention to DRM, so much so that Sustainable Development Goal (SDG) #17.1 tracks country-level domestic revenue efforts.[31] More generally, taxation is a core function of the state as it contributes to the social contract between the latter and citizens.[32] Previous studies suggest that this relationship is particularly important in developing countries where state building should rely on the government's ability to raise taxes.[33] It is estimated that the average additional spending to achieve SDGs in five key areas (education, health, roads, electricity, and water) in low-income countries (LICs) by 2030 would be 15.4% of gross domestic product (GDP).[34] In the average low-income country (LIC), over and above the current revenue collections, 5 additional percentage points of revenue (as a percentage of GDP) would have to come from domestic taxes. As these estimates only cover five areas, it is likely the actual amounts would be substantially larger if all SDGs were to be provided for. Many developing countries have tax-to-GDP ratios well below 13%,[35] which is the minimum tax-to-GDP ratio needed to achieve a significant acceleration in growth,[36] and considerably below what is necessary to fully fund the SDGs. Therefore, besides the growing recognition of the importance of taxation for growth and redistribution, DRM is all the more critical for supporting higher essential spending.[37] Mobilizing more domestic resources is also vital for maintaining debt sustainability when external debt payments are rising.[38] Moreover,

---

30 M. Moore. 2013. Obstacles to Increasing Tax Revenues in Low Income Countries. ICTD Working Paper 15. Brighton: International Centre for Tax and Development. https://www.ictd.ac/publication/obstacles-to-increasing-tax-revenues-in-low-income-countries/. | T. Besley and T. Persson. 2014. Why Do Developing Countries Tax So Little? Journal of Economic Perspectives. 28(4). pp. 99–120. American Economic Association. November. https://www.researchgate.net/publication/268884638_Why_Do_Developing_Countries_Tax_So_Little. | M. Forstater. 2018. Publishing tax strategies: meaningful or boilerplate? *Tax Journal*, 31. pp. 16–17. Lexis Nexis. 30 August. https://www.taxjournal.com/articles/publishing-tax-strategies-meaningful-or-boilerplate-30082018.

31 In July 2015, the Third UN Conference on Financing for Development in Ethiopia agreed to the Addis Ababa Action Agenda, aimed at addressing the challenges of financing and creating an enabling environment for sustainable development. This agreement included measures to assist developing countries in setting nationally defined revenue targets and timelines for enhancing revenues and supporting countries in reaching these targets. | United Nations. 2015. Outcome document adopted at the Third International Conference on Financing for Development (Addis Ababa Action Agenda). New York. https://www.un.org/development/desa/financing/sites/www.un.org.development. desa.financing/files/2021-09/AAAA_Outcome.pdf.

32 Laura Paler. 2013. Keeping the Public Purse: An Experiment in Windfalls, Taxes, and the Incentives to Restrain Government. *American Political Science Review*, 107(4), 706–25. https://www.cambridge.org/core/journals/american-political-science-review/article/abs/keeping-the-public-purse-an-experiment-in-windfalls-taxes-and-the-incentives-to-restrain-government/1015EC29926C5ADD82C14FFECC582A4D.

33 D.A. Bräutigam. 2008. Introduction: Taxation and State-building in Developing Countries. In D. Bräutigam, O-H Fjelstad, and M. Moore, eds. *Taxation and State-building in Developing Countries: Capacity and Consent*. pp. 1–33. Cambridge: Cambridge University Press. | T. Besley and T. Persson. 2011. Fragile States and Development Policy. *Journal of the European Economic Association*. 9(3). pp. 371–398. Wiley. June. https://www.researchgate.net/publication/227500383_Fragile_States_and_Development_Policy.

34 V. Gaspar et al. 2019. Fiscal Policy and Development: Human, Social, and Physical Investment for the SDGs. *IMF Staff Discussion Notes*. Note No. 2019/003. Washington, DC: International Monetary Fund. 23 January. https://www.imf.org/en/Publications/Staff-Discussion-Notes/ Issues/2019/01/18/Fiscal-Policy-and-Development-Human-Social-and-Physical-Investments-for-the-SDGs-46444.

35 According to World Economic Outlook data, Timor-Leste registered tax revenues of 6.23% of GDP in 2020.

36 V. Gaspar, L. Jaramillo, and P. Wingender. 2016. Tax Capacity and Growth: Is There a Tipping Point? *IMF Working Papers*. Paper No. 2016/234. Washington, DC: International Monetary Fund. 2 December. https://www.imf.org/en/Publications/WP/Issues/2016/12/31/Tax-Capacity-and-Growth-Is-there-a-Tipping-Point-44436.

37 C. Lane and E. Harris. 2018. Mounting Debt Threatens Sustainable Development Goals. International Monetary Fund Blog, Available at https://blogs.imf.org/2018/04/27/debt-as-an-obstacle-to-the-sustainable-development-goals/. | Footnote 34.

38 Since 2011, average external debt payments have increased gradually in LICs, to an average of 12.4% of government revenue by 2019, a rise of 125%. Growing principal and interest payments on general government debt have also crowded-out public spending. Refer to, T. Jones. 2020. Rising Debt Burdens, the Impact on Public Spending, and the Coronavirus Crisis. CGD Policy Paper 199. Washington, DC: Center for Global Development. 10 December. https://www.cgdev.org/sites/default/files/PP197-Jones-LICs-Debt.pdf. | J. Hurley. 2018. The Importance of Domestic Resource Mobilization for Debt Sustainability. Center for Global Development. 28 March. https://www.cgdev.org/blog/ importance-domestic-resource-mobilization-debt-sustainability.

broadening and deepening the tax base can serve as a catalyst for broader improvements in government accountability, responsiveness, and institutional capacity.[39]

Furthermore, DRM has taken on greater urgency given the COVID-19 pandemic crisis and its impact on both revenues and expenditures. Countries increased spending on health to protect lives as well as to provide support to households and businesses through direct transfers and/or tax relief. Also, the reduction in economic activity considerably lowered revenue collections in LICs in 2020 (Figure 9). There is a strong likelihood that the crisis will leave a permanent impact on the structures of these economies, with important implications for the tax base. Experience from the global financial crisis of 2008–2010 suggests that severe output contractions are associated with falling tax compliance.[40] The International Monetary Fund (IMF) has recently estimated that scarring from the COVID-19 pandemic would increase the already sizable financing needs to achieve the SDGs.[41]

Figure 9: Tax Revenue Projection Pre- and Post-Pandemic for 2020 in Low-Income Countries

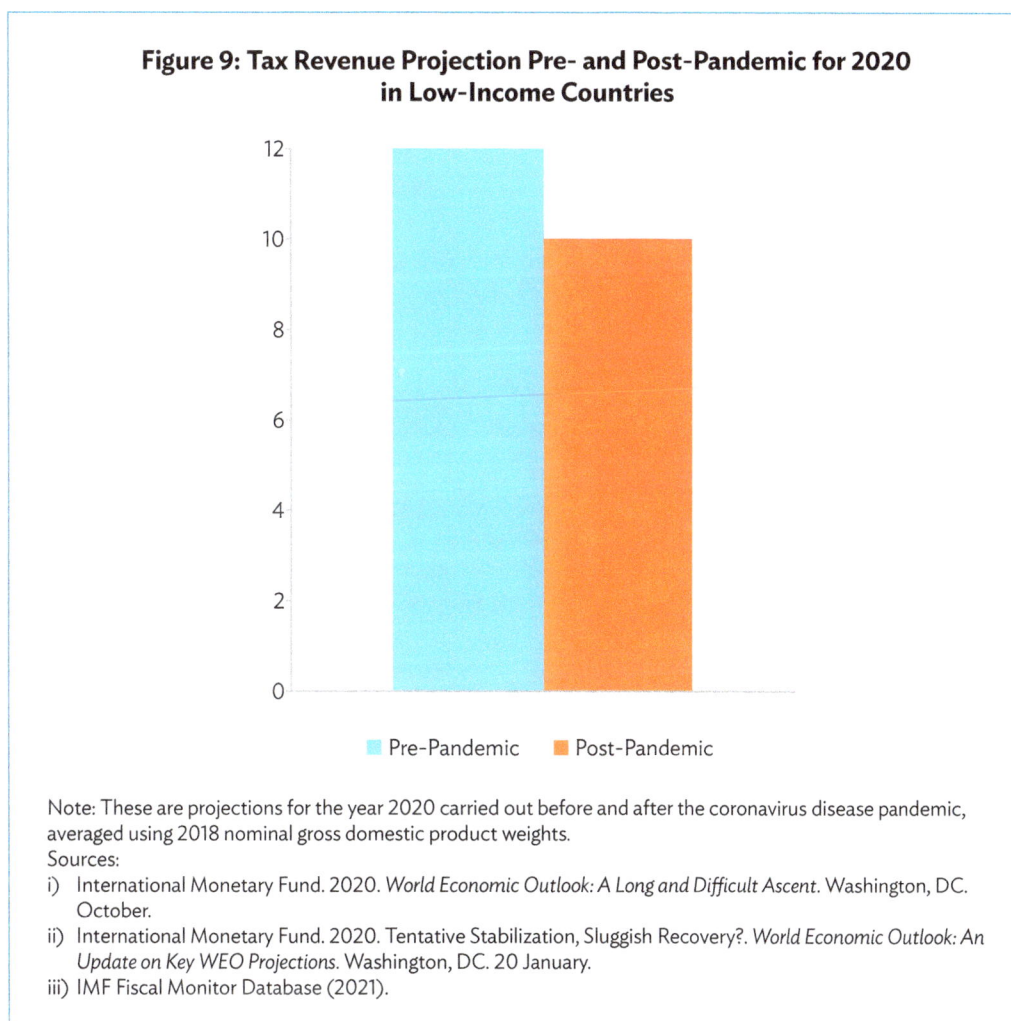

Note: These are projections for the year 2020 carried out before and after the coronavirus disease pandemic, averaged using 2018 nominal gross domestic product weights.
Sources:
i)   International Monetary Fund. 2020. *World Economic Outlook: A Long and Difficult Ascent*. Washington, DC. October.
ii) International Monetary Fund. 2020. Tentative Stabilization, Sluggish Recovery?. *World Economic Outlook: An Update on Key WEO Projections*. Washington, DC. 20 January.
iii) IMF Fiscal Monitor Database (2021).

---

39   Footnote 33 (2nd citation).
40   J.D. Brondolo. 2009. Collecting Taxes During an Economic Crisis: Challenges and Policy Options. *IMF Staff Position Notes*. No. 2019/017. Washington, DC: International Monetary Fund. 14 July. https://www.imf.org/en/Publications/IMF-Staff-Position-Notes/Issues/2016/12/31/Collecting-Taxes-During-an-Economic-Crisis-Challenges-and-Policy-Options-23092.
41   D. Benedek et al. 2021. A Post-Pandemic Assessment of the Sustainable Development Goals. *IMF Staff Discussion Notes*. No. 2021/003. Washington, DC: International Monetary Fund. 27 April. https://www.imf.org/en/Publications/Staff-Discussion-Notes/Issues/2021/04/27/A-Post-Pandemic-Assessment-of-the-Sustainable-Development-Goals-460076.

While many tax systems in developing countries, including Timor-Leste, conform to global benchmarks, policymakers have to deal with challenges of poor revenue collections in spite of high tax rates and the reforms in their tax systems.[42] Against this background, to formally provide an assessment of tax policy in Timor-Leste, a wide array of possible aspects can be looked at. The three focused on here are i) tax capacity and potential, ii) tax buoyancy, and iii) tax productivity.

B. Assessing Tax Capacity and Potential

This section deals with the concept and empirical estimation of Asia's taxable capacity and tax potential.[43] Taxable capacity as a concept is much-debated and yet, of great practical importance. Tax capacity (or the tax frontier) is defined as the maximum theoretical level of tax revenues that a country can mobilize given its structural characteristics. The ratio of actual tax revenue to tax capacity is labeled as tax effort. The difference between current revenue and tax capacity can be interpreted as the tax potential, which reflects policy factors, such as low tax rates and narrow tax bases (i.e., high level of tax exemptions and deductions) or inefficient tax collection (i.e., a high level of noncompliance). Of course, policy factors could also reflect societal preference for a small government and low provision of public goods.[44]

Measuring the tax performance of countries is both theoretically and practically challenging.[45] Calculating tax effort and actual tax collection benchmarks allows us to classify countries into four groups: (i) low tax collection, low tax effort; (ii) high tax collection, high tax effort; (iii) low tax collection, high tax effort; and (iv) high tax collection, low tax effort. This classification is based on the global average of tax collection and a tax effort index of 1, corresponding to a country where tax collection is the same as estimated taxable capacity. We argue that countries at various stages of development and with different initial levels of tax collection and effort should rely on different strategies for tax reforms.

Table 1 presents the estimation of tax capacity, tax effort, and tax potential for Asian economies for which data are available over the period 1990–2019. It shows that most Asian economies have space to increase revenue. With a few exceptions, results are in line with priors and previous estimates.[46] According to the truncated-normal model, the difference between tax capacity and current revenue is 4.2% of GDP on average. According to the half-normal model, this difference is 4.0% of GDP.[47] There are wide variations across countries with a standard deviation of tax potential of around 4.5% of GDP in both models. Countries with similar revenue levels can have very different levels of effort. This is the case for India and Thailand or Papua New Guinea and Singapore, for example. Timor-Leste, in particular, is placed within the rectangle of low tax collection and low tax effort. This result is in line with World Bank's 2021 report which states that with Timor-Leste's tax collection being significantly below its full potential, there seems to exist ample scope for tax policy and administration reforms.[48] What these results do not shed light on, however, is precisely how this capacity can be increased.

---

42 R. Junquera-Varela et al. 2017. *Strengthening Domestic Resource Mobilization: Moving from Theory to Practice in Low- and Middle-Income Countries*. Washington, DC: World Bank. https://openknowledge.worldbank.org/handle/10986/27265. | The international community has recognized the pressing need for developing countries to expand fiscal space. | O-H Fjelstad. 2014. Tax and development: Donor support to strengthen tax systems in developing countries. *Public Administration and Development*. 34 (3). pp. 182–193. 5 August. https://doi.org/10.1002/pad.1676. | More recently, the donor community has intensified efforts as part of the "billions to trillions" drive to mobilize resources to meet the sustainable development goals. | E. Mawdsley. 2018. From billions to trillions: Financing the SDGs in a world 'beyond aid'. *Dialogues in Human Geography*. 8 (2). pp. 191–195. Sage Publishing. 8 July. https://doi.org/10.1177/2043820618780789.

43 To have an estimate of where Timor-Leste lies in this regard a wider sample or comparator is necessary. | Asia is used.

44 C. Pessino and R. Fenochietto. 2013. Understanding Countries' Tax Effort, *IMF Working Paper*, vol. 13244.

45 Tax capacity in this study was estimated using a stochastic frontier model based on country characteristics, such as per capita income, inequality, the share of government spending on education, the sector composition of the economy, and institutional factors such as indicators of governance. Also see, J. Torres. 2013. Revenue and Expenditure Gaps and Fiscal Consolidation: A Cross-Country Analysis. *IMF Working Papers*. No. WP/05/xx, Washington, DC: International Monetary Front. https://www.banrep.gov.co/sites/default/files/publicaciones/archivos/sem_309.pdf. | Technical details underlying the values shown in Table 1 are provided in Appendix 3.

46 Footnote 4. | International Monetary Fund. 2013. Fiscal Monitor: Taxing Times. World Economic and Financial Surveys. October.

47 While exercising extreme caution, upon comparing earlier IMF results with those presented here, it appears that tax effort in Asia has improved in recent years.

48 World Bank. 2021. *Timor-Leste Public Expenditure Review: Changing Course Towards Better and More Sustainable Spending*. Washington, DC: World Bank. https://openknowledge.worldbank.org/handle/10986/36502.

Table 1: Tax Potential in Asia: Tax Capacity–Current Tax Revenue

(i) Low Tax Collection, Low Tax Effort

Economies	Current Tax Revenue (% GDP)	Tax Effort	Tax Capacity	Tax Potential
Indonesia	11	0.60	18.38	7.38
Malaysia	12	0.43	28.14	16.14
Singapore	13	0.58	22.47	9.47
Pakistan	12	0.54	22.12	10.12
Viet Nam	14	0.82	17.13	3.13
Cambodia	17	0.8	21.31	4.31
India	17	0.82	20.63	3.63
Thailand	17	0.55	30.97	13.97
Philippines	18	0.75	23.86	5.86
Timor-Leste	7.6	0.58	13.16	5.56

(ii) High Tax Collection, High Tax Effort

Countries	Current Tax Revenue (% GDP)	Tax Effort	Tax Capacity	Tax Potential
Federated States of Micronesia	35	0.99	35.43	0.43
Republic of Korea	27	0.99	27.34	0.34
Samoa	26	0.98	26.57	0.57
Solomon Islands	26	0.99	26.32	0.32
PRC	24	0.99	24.3	0.3
Fiji	24	0.92	26.07	2.07
Tonga	20	0.99	20.25	0.25

(iii) Low Tax Collection, High Tax Effort

Economies	Current Tax Revenue (% GDP)	Tax Effort	Tax Capacity	Tax Potential
Papua New Guinea	13	0.99	13.16	0.16
Hong Kong, China	14	0.99	14.17	0.17
Myanmar	7	0.91	7.7	0.7
Lao PDR	12	0.99	12.15	0.15
Vanuatu	17	0.97	17.47	0.47

(iv) High Tax Collection, Low Tax Effort

Countries	Current Tax Revenue (% GDP)	Tax Effort	Tax Capacity	Tax Potential
Japan	33	0.78	42.31	9.31
New Zealand	33	0.82	40.13	7.13
Australia	29	0.76	37.97	8.97

GDP = gross domestic product , Lao PDR = Lao People's Democratic Republic, PRC = People's Republic of China.
Notes:
1. Estimation based on International Monetary Fund tax and macroeconomic data for the period 1990–2019.
2. "Current tax revenue" includes social security contributions.
Source: Author's computations.

Figure 10 plots the average tax capacity, average tax revenue collected, and average tax effort for different subgroups within developing Asia. Note that Timor-Leste is part of ADB's Southeast Asia region.[49] Looking at Figure 10, South Asia has the lowest tax capacity and actual tax collection, even though it is in Southeast Asia where the tax effort is the lowest (with the exception of Timor-Leste). The Pacific region seems to have the highest tax effort while East

49 The subregional groupings in this report differ from ADB's subregional operational groupings—South Asia (Afghanistan, Bangladesh, Bhutan, India, Maldives, Nepal, Pakistan, and Sri Lanka); Southeast Asia (Cambodia, Indonesia, Lao PDR, Myanmar, Philippines, Thailand, Timor-Leste, and Viet Nam); East Asia (Hong Kong, China; Mongolia; PRC; Republic of Korea; and Taipei,China). ADB's regular operations in Afghanistan and Myanmar have been on hold since August and February 2021, respectively. | ADB. 2021. ADB Statement on Afghanistan. News Release. 10 November. https://www.adb.org/news/adb-statement-afghanistan; and ADB. 2021. ADB Statement on Myanmar. News release. 10 March. https://www.adb.org/news/adb-statement-myanmar.

Asia has the highest tax capacity. These results suggest that the tax potential (that is, the difference between actual tax collections and tax capacity) is highest in Pakistan, Malaysia, and Thailand and lowest in Timor-Leste, Papua New Guinea, and the Lao People's Democratic Republic (Lao PDR).

Ultimately, policy-wise, countries with a low level of actual tax collection and low tax effort (e.g., Thailand or Singapore) may have more room to increase tax revenues in order to reach their taxable capacity without causing major economic distortions or costs. On the other hand, Asian countries with a low level of tax collection but high tax effort (e.g., Timor-Leste or the Lao PDR) have less opportunity to increase tax revenues (without possibly creating distortions or high compliance costs). Note that these results should be interpreted with caution due to caveats in the modeling of tax capacity and effort. The foregoing panel analysis needs to be complemented with a detailed analysis of Timor-Leste's tax system (that is, tax policy instruments and revenue administration), taking into consideration the country's overall fiscal policy, public expenditure needs, and the overall level of development. This is beyond the scope of this note.

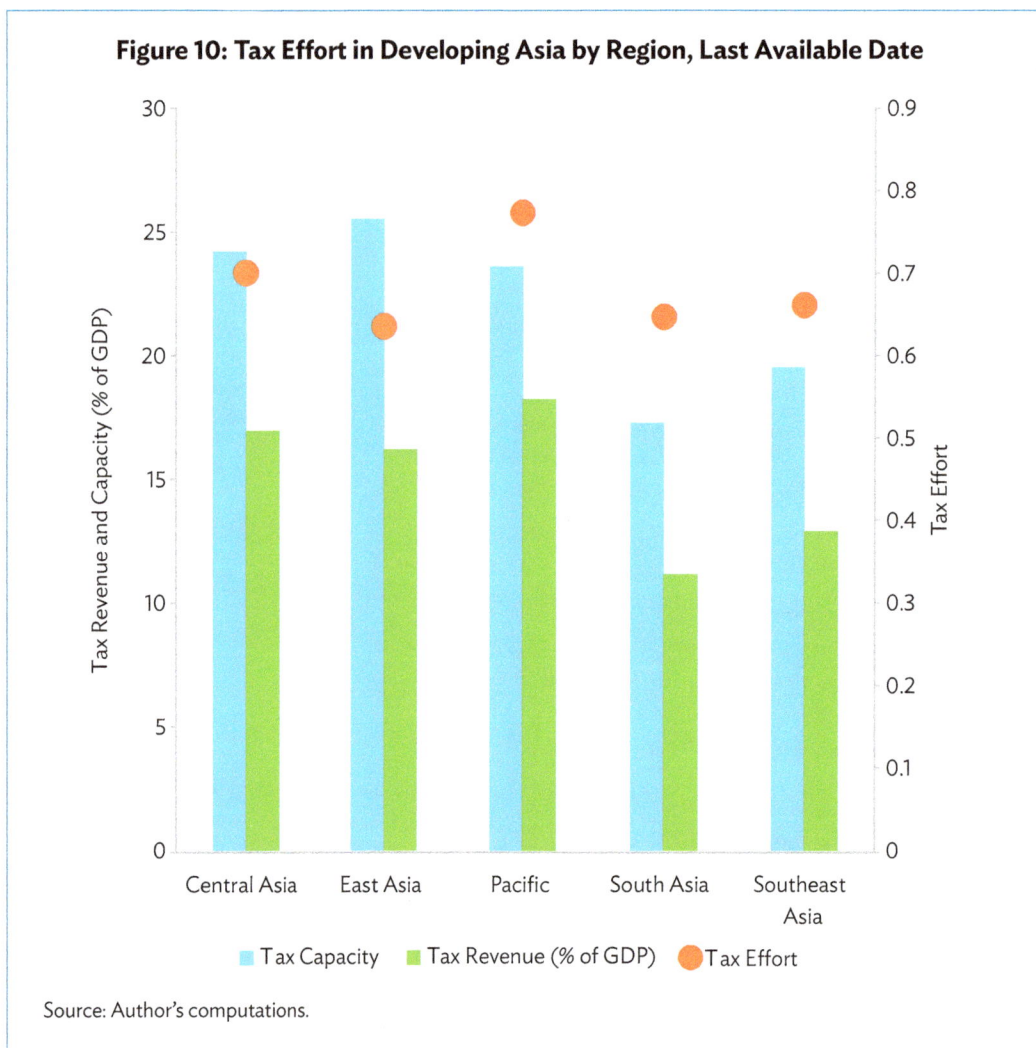

Figure 10: Tax Effort in Developing Asia by Region, Last Available Date

Source: Author's computations.

C. Assessing the Degree of Tax Buoyancy

Countries have attempted to lift growth by increasing public expenditure. This is a salient characteristic of Timor-Leste (as already mentioned)—most of its growth over the past couple of decades has come primarily from expansionary government spending. That said, Timor-Leste, like many other developing countries, has not been able to mobilize revenues through taxation to match the rise in government spends. The answer to whether greater growth in the future will raise revenue and allow keeping the fiscal balances in check depends on the buoyancy of the tax system, which is a measure of how tax revenues vary with changes in output.[50] A buoyancy greater than unity over the long-run is a desirable feature of a tax system if there is increasing demand for public services and if a country would like to pursue relative financial stability. If buoyancy is low, discretionary changes may make up for it but any impact from such changes can be lagged and disproportionally high.[51]

Why is looking at this issue important? An examination of tax buoyancy is crucial for tax policy formulation and design for two reasons. First, tax buoyancy illustrates the role that revenue policy plays in ensuring fiscal sustainability in the long-run and in stabilizing the economy over the business cycle in the short-run.[52] Second, assessing country-specific tax buoyancy allows us to ascertain if the government is keeping tax mobilization in line with economic activity, and estimating individual tax buoyancies helps identify the weak and strong spots of the revenue system. Such analyses allow fiscal authorities (i) to ascertain if more effort should be put into mobilizing revenues, and (ii) to better direct this effort at increasing the share of those taxes that better respond to a sustained increase in income.[53]

In this subsection, the following question is raised: how large are tax buoyancies in Timor-Leste and other similar emerging and developing Asian countries both over the long and in the short run? To answer this question, annual tax revenue data for an unbalanced panel of 22 emerging and developing Asian countries between 1990 and 2019 is used. Details of the country-specific estimates are presented in Table 2. The average long-run buoyancy estimate is 1.15 while the corresponding short-run buoyancy is 1.72. Timor-Leste (together with Bhutan, Myanmar, India, Nepal, Solomon Islands, and the People's Republic of China) displays long-run buoyancy that is statistically significantly higher than 1. This means that for Timor-Leste, growth has improved fiscal sustainability over time. In several countries but not Timor-Leste (e.g. Bangladesh, Brunei Darussalam, Maldives, the Philippines, and Thailand), the tax system has acted as a good automatic stabilizer as evidenced by short-run buoyancies statistically larger than 1. For Timor-Leste, the tax system is mostly neither good nor bad as an automatic stabilizer (this confirms the findings in Table 2A in the Appendix on fiscal stabilization).

Table 2: Overall Tax Buoyancy by Country, Emerging and Developing Asia

Estimation type	Panel Estimation		
Countries	Long-Run Buoyancy	Short-Run Buoyancy	Speed of Adjustment
Timor-Leste	1.245***	1.074***	-0.554***
Maldives	1.308***	1.729***	-0.148
Bangladesh	1.019***	2.393***	-0.316
Bhutan	1.328***	2.320***	-0.557***
Brunei Darussalam	1.465***	2.878***	-0.240**

50 See Appendix 4 for technical details.
51 O.J. Blanchard, G. Dell'Aricia, and P. Mauro. 2010. Rethinking Macroeconomic Policy. *IMF Staff Position Notes.* No. 2010/003. Washington, DC: International Monetary Fund. 12 February. https://www.imf.org/en/Publications/IMF-Staff-Position-Notes/Issues/2016/12/31/Rethinking-Macroeconomic-Policy-23513.
52 Buoyancy estimates could in principle capture both an automatic stabilizer component as well as discretionary policy changes. Due to lack of sufficient and long-term information on tax components, a separate analysis by tax-policy instrument was not possible to carry out.
53 S. Gupta, J. T. Jalles, and J. Liu. 2022. Tax Buoyancy in Sub-Saharan Africa and its Determinants. *International Tax and Public Finance.* 29. pp. 890–921. Springer Nature. 21 September. https://doi.org/10.1007/s10797-021-09694-x.

Estimation type	Panel Estimation		
Countries	Long-Run Buoyancy	Short-Run Buoyancy	Speed of Adjustment
Myanmar	**1.255***	**0.416**	-0.316***
India	**1.090***	**1.589***	-0.389
Indonesia	**1.058***	**1.234***	-0.291
Lao People's Democratic Republic	**1.319***	**1.344***	0.101
Nepal	**1.425***	**1.946***	-0.492*
Philippines	**1.092***	**2.032***	-0.160
Thailand	**1.094***	**1.561***	-0.356
Viet Nam	**0.967***	**1.441***	-0.341*
Solomon Islands	**1.410***	**2.545***	-0.231*
Kiribati	**0.904***	**0.110**	-0.219*
Vanuatu	**1.009***	**1.855***	-0.488***
Papua New Guinea	**0.941***	**1.223***	-0.146
Tonga	**1.137***	**1.533***	-0.373**
Marshall Islands	**0.803***	**1.256***	-0.296*
Federated States of Micronesia	**1.502***	**4.291***	-0.778***
Tuvalu	**0.511***	**2.356***	-1.567***
People's Republic of China	**1.358***	**0.671***	0.207**
Mean	1.147	1.718	
Median	1.116	1.575	
Standard Deviation	0.243	0.895	

Notes:
1. Bold means statistically not different from 1 at 5% level.
2. * denotes statistical significance at the 10% level.
3. ** denotes statistical significance at the 5% level.
4. *** denotes statistical significance at the 1% level.

Source: Author's computations.

The subsection also examines variations in the stabilization role of taxation during periods of economic expansion and contraction. Results are shown in Table 3. Buoyancy is generally larger during times of economic expansions than during recessions. This result contradicts those reported by Furceri and Jalles (2018) who found that the overall impact of fiscal stabilization (measured with a proxy of the degree of fiscal counter-cyclicality) was larger during recessionary periods.[54]

---

54   D. Furceri and J. Jalles. 2018. Determinants and Effects of Fiscal Counter-Cyclicality. *Ensayos sobre Política Económica*. 36. 137–151. 10.32468/ Espe.8508.

Table 3: Asymmetric Short-Term Buoyancy over the Business Cycle, Timor-Leste

Type of Revenue	Economic Expansion	Economic Recession
Approach	STAR based on Real GDP Growth	
Tax Revenues	0.821*	0.534
	(0.394)	(1.048)

GDP = gross domestic product, STAR = smooth transition autoregressive.
Notes:
1. Estimation of Equation (E8).
2. Standard errors in parenthesis.
3. * denotes statistical significance at the 10% level.
4. ** denotes statistical significance at the 5% level.
5. *** denotes statistical significance at the 1% level.
Source: Author's computations.

To test the stability of these results over time, equation D4 (in Appendix 4) was generalized by introducing the assumption that the regression coefficients may vary over time. Figure 4A in Appendix 4 shows the interquartile range for the same sample of Asian economies for the case of the overall tax buoyancy. In general, buoyancy has been increasing over time and converging among the economies in the sample. Both indirect taxes and other taxes seem to have contributed to this increase over time while direct taxes have had a downward trend since 2015. Overall, this is good and promising news going forward.

D. Tax Productivity and Tax Efficiency

In addition to tax ratios, a tax system's performance can also be viewed across economies by contrasting the relative productivity of individual taxes, most often the value-added tax (VAT) and the corporate income tax (CIT).[55] There are several measures that can be used for this purpose, one of which is the productivity ratio, which measures how much each percentage point of the standard tax rate collects in terms of GDP.[56] Comparisons of this ratio over time or across countries can be used to gauge the relative revenue performance of a given tax. A low ratio is typically taken as evidence of weak design or enforcement.[57]

In Figure 11, panel a shows the box-whisker results of the CIT productivity ratio for different income groups, while panel b provides a more detailed assessment of countries within developing Asia.[58] This measure gives an indication of how much revenue is raised by each percentage point of the CIT rate. The overall picture for developing Asia shows a higher median ratio compared to both Latin America and the Caribbean (LAC) countries and advanced economies. Timor-Leste occupies the worst position out of those countries with available data (extreme left).

---

55   S. Gupta and J. T. Jalles. 2022b. Priorities for strengthening key revenue sources in Asia. Background paper prepared for the report *Asian Development Outlook 2022: Mobilizing Taxes for Development*. Asian Development Bank. Manila. https://www.adb.org/sites/default/files/institutional-document/782851/ado2022bp-strengthening-revenue-sources-asia.pdf.
56   The productivity of a given tax reflects how broad its tax base is.
57   The revenue productivity measure does not, however, give insight into the relative contribution of these factors.
58   The paper focuses on revenue productivity for the CIT as this is the only tax component for which there is detailed information on Timor-Leste. Brunei Darussalam and the Marshall Islands were removed for being outliers with very high ratios.

Figure 11: Corporate Income Tax Productivity Ratio (Top Combined Rate)

a. By Region

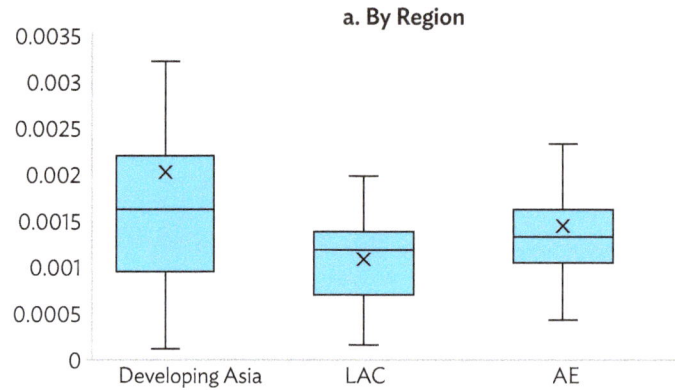

b. By Country in Asia

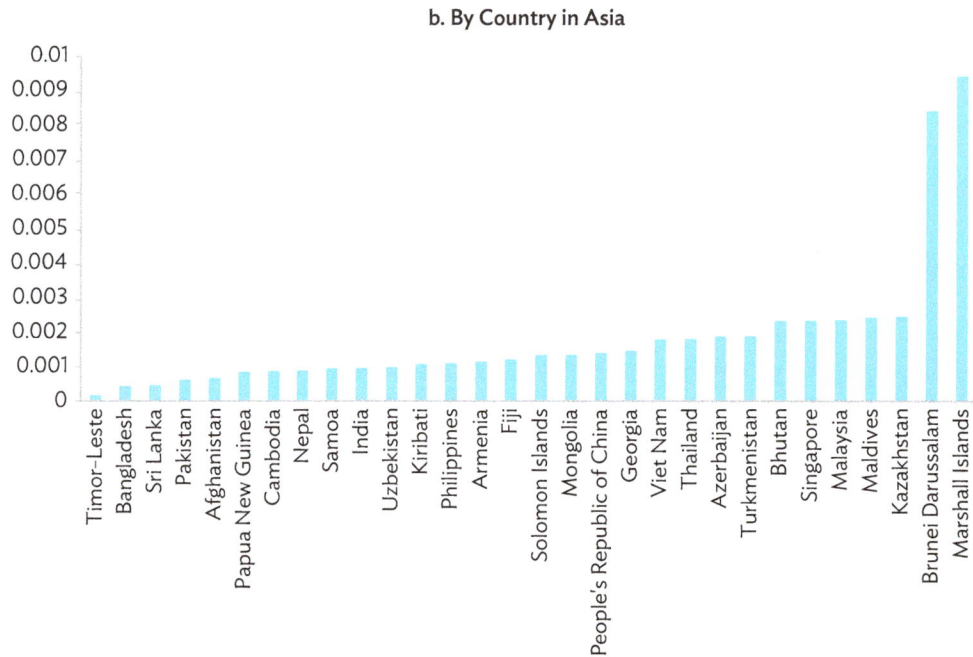

AE = advanced economies, CIT = corporate income tax, LAC = Latin America and the Caribbean.

Notes:
1. CIT Productivity is calculated as (CIT Revenue) / [(CIT Rate) * (GDP)].
2. Box-whisker diagrams calculated with data from the last available year.
3. Bar charts calculated with average data between 2000 and the last available year.

Source: Author's calculations using IMF data.

IV IDENTIFICATION OF FISCAL CHALLENGES AND PRIORITIES

There are several challenges ahead for the post-pandemic recovery phase in Timor-Leste. The Timorese state must develop its capacity to respond, first and foremost, to the urgent needs of the population. It can do this more effectively by i) creating conditions for stronger and more resilient growth and ii) rapidly strengthening the soundness of public finances by diversifying revenue sources away from oil-related ones. This will create more fiscal space for developmental purposes. These objectives can be achieved by grabbing the momentum to engage in long-needed structural (including tax) reforms that can propel growth in an inclusive manner. This will be the focus in what follows below.

A. Work toward Restructuring the Economy

The World Bank notes that the underlying economic policy challenge for Timor-Leste is how to best use its oil and gas wealth to lift the non-oil economy onto a higher growth path and reduce poverty.[59] The prospect of declining income from the sovereign wealth fund requires government plans for economic diversification. This is essential in view of the country´s depleting oil revenues, inadequate infrastructure, low productive capacity, and youth unemployment. Timor-Leste faces structural challenges that limit growth, constrain public service delivery, and hinder private sector development. In fact, the non-oil private sector economy remains underdeveloped.[60]

A diversification and internationalization strategy requires a comprehensive and coherent view of the different options and associated policy settings. This should be part of a nationwide strategic developmental plan that should assemble different ministries and the international donor community. The possible strategies are schematically described in Figure 12. First, the split between tradable and non-tradable sectors is determined by trade policy and the level of relative prices. Second, non-tradable sectors require particular attention in terms of competition and regulatory environment precisely because they are sheltered from foreign competition. Moreover, tradable activities use many service inputs, so their competitiveness also depends on the performance of those non-tradable sectors. The Timorese economy needs to rebalance its productive structure toward non-oil and nonfood tradable sectors and, concomitantly, increase the productivity of their domestic value-added content whose performance has been severely limited in recent decades. A large part of the productivity catching-up potential in a small open economy such as Timor-Leste is associated with tradable sectors.[61]

Another related challenge before the Timorese economy, currently dominated by the public sector, is to allow the private sector to play a much greater role in the future. In fact, research shows that typically in most countries there is complementarity between public and private spending which are beneficial to aggregate demand.[62] To date, the private sector in Timor-Leste has only made a limited contribution to growth due to the lack of an enabling environment and a weak investment climate. Not only does the state fragility status of Timor-Leste reduce the volume of investments

---

59 Footnote 19 (1st citation).
60 Footnote 7.
61 Moreover, there is evidence that labor productivity tends to be higher in tradable sectors. According to Rodrik (2013), industry (and, by extension, tradable sectors) can also provide an unconditional convergence mechanism, meaning that they are less dependent on specific country factors related to endowments (physical and human) or the quality of institutions. | D. Rodrik. 2013. Unconditional Convergence in Manufacturing. *The Quarterly Journal of Economics.* 128 (1). pp. 165–204. Oxford University Press. https://doi.org/10.1093/qje/qjs047.
62 J. T. Jalles and G. Karras. 2021. Private and public consumption: substitutes or complements? *Oxford Economic Papers,* 74 (3). pp. 805–819. Oxford University Press. 10 September. https://doi.org/10.1093/oep/gpab049. Jalles and Karras find that private and government consumption are best described as complementary both in the aggregate and for nine different categories of government spending. The degree of complementarity, however, differs substantially across government spending categories, being the highest for education, recreation, and housing in countries belonging to the Organisation for Economic Co-operation and Development (OECD), and for public order and recreation in the non-OECD countries.

Figure 12: Sector Specialization Strategies and Associated Policy Settings

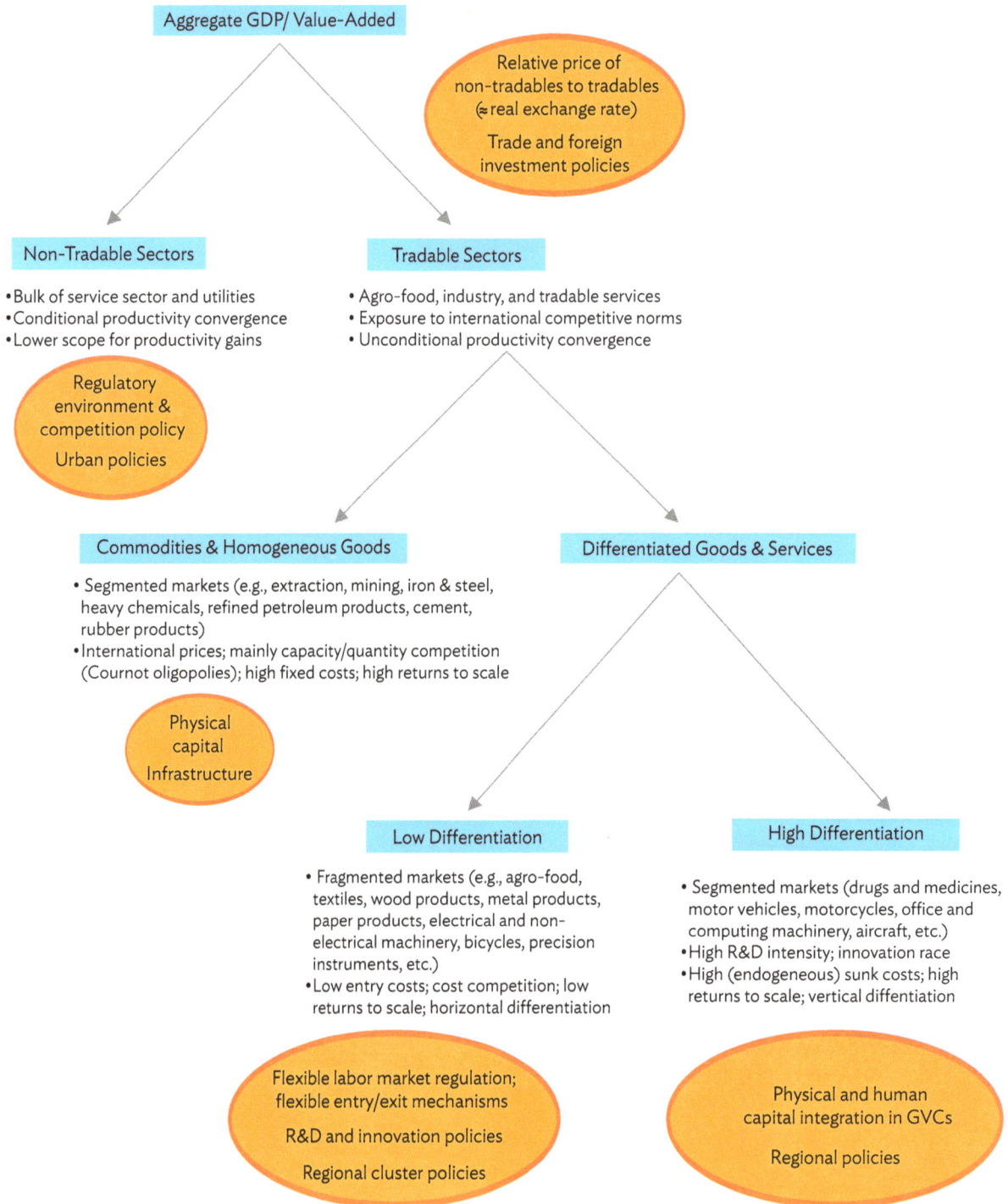

Aggregate GDP/ Value-Added

Relative price of non-tradables to tradables (≈ real exchange rate)

Trade and foreign investment policies

Non-Tradable Sectors

• Bulk of service sector and utilities
• Conditional productivity convergence
• Lower scope for productivity gains

Regulatory environment & competition policy

Urban policies

Tradable Sectors

• Agro-food, industry, and tradable services
• Exposure to international competitive norms
• Unconditional productivity convergence

Commodities & Homogeneous Goods

• Segmented markets (e.g., extraction, mining, iron & steel, heavy chemicals, refined petroleum products, cement, rubber products)
• International prices; mainly capacity/quantity competition (Cournot oligopolies); high fixed costs; high returns to scale

Physical capital

Infrastructure

Differentiated Goods & Services

Low Differentiation

• Fragmented markets (e.g., agro-food, textiles, wood products, metal products, paper products, electrical and non-electrical machinery, bicycles, precision instruments, etc.)
• Low entry costs; cost competition; low returns to scale; horizontal differentiation

Flexible labor market regulation; flexible entry/exit mechanisms

R&D and innovation policies

Regional cluster policies

High Differentiation

• Segmented markets (drugs and medicines, motor vehicles, motorcycles, office and computing machinery, aircraft, etc.)
• High R&D intensity; innovation race
• High (endogeneous) sunk costs; high returns to scale; vertical diffentiation

Physical and human capital integration in GVCs

Regional policies

GDP = gross domestic product, GVC = global value chain, R&D = research and development.
Source: Author's analysis.

(especially foreign direct investments), it also affects the composition of investments by tilting incentives toward the accumulation of less specialized capital goods that have lower returns, but can be easily divested in response to fragility shocks.[63] The ease with which these investments could be divested or reallocated constitutes a source of macroeconomic volatility. Community efforts to rebuild and strengthen their livelihoods will be constrained unless private investment recreates markets and generates employment.[64] An essential part of achieving stability involves people:[65] quickly empowering Timorese local entrepreneurs and investors can create a dynamic and growing private sector and improve the local power dynamics. A stronger Timor-Leste needs to be particularly creative in soliciting the return of private investment by improving the overall institutional and business environment. Note that in a flourishing private sector setting, formal businesses also provide the government with the tax revenue necessary to fund social services and infrastructure needs.[66] In addition, private businesses can provide financial support for local security programs, social programs and sociocultural programs which can help in alleviating poverty concerns.[67] For countries transitioning toward prosperity such as Timor-Leste, governments need to play a wide range of stabilizing functions for which they often lack sufficient capacity. The private sector can help close some of these critical gaps. Critical infrastructure can also be funded by the private sector through public–private partnerships.[68] However, an underpinning legal framework is needed for such transactions to materialize, coupled with adequate tendering processes, competition, and transparency. Otherwise, there is a high risk of elite capture and poor value to government (and ultimately populations).

B. Build Conditions for a Post-Pandemic Reform Momentum

Although the pandemic may be thought of as a factor in Timor-Leste's slowdown or stagnation, the slowdown in potential growth started earlier (recall Figure 3 panel c). This suggests that deeper structural factors have been at play. Good post-pandemic macroeconomic performance requires a sequential approach to reforms as these will help both short-run recovery and medium- to long-run potential growth catching-up. There exists a consensus on the desirability of making markets more efficient to increase productivity, increasing international competitiveness and employment, and improving future growth prospects.[69] Structural reforms can be motivated by multiple policy objectives.[70] Building

---

63 H. Wolf. 2005. Volatility: Definitions and Consequences. In J. Aizenman and B. Pinto, eds. *Managing Economic Volatility and Crises: A Practitioner's Guide.* Chapter 1. Cambridge University Press. https://doi.org/10.1017/CBO9780511510755.004.

64 T. Addison, ed. 2003. *From Conflict to Recovery in Africa.* New York: Oxford University Press Inc.

65 International Finance Corporation. 2019. Generating Private Investment in Fragile and Conflict-Affected Areas. Washington, DC. https://www.ifc.org/wps/wcm/connect/07cb32dd-d775-4577-9d5f-d254cc52b61a/201902-IFC-FCS-Study.pdf?MOD=AJPERES.

66 In 2015, in Afghanistan, the revenue from the taxes on goods and services paid by private firms corresponded to four times the total net assistance provided by development agencies.

67 In Sri Lanka, business associations created initiatives to bring the businesses of different ethnic groups together. In Colombia, businesses worked on urban employment programs and related education and social services.

68 An example of this is the Liberia Electricity Corporation. In coordination with other development partners, the International Finance Corporation (IFC) structured a partnership between the Government of Liberia and a private partner, which expanded the reach of affordable electricity from 500 connections to ultimately serve 165,000 Liberians. In FCAS, telecommunications network improvements are also often driven by private investment. In Afghanistan, for example, mobile cellular telephone subscriptions increased from less than 1 per 100 citizens in 2003 to over 60 per 100 by 2015. In Sierra Leone, the subscription rate improved from 2.4 in 2003 to 89.5 per 100 citizens by 2015.

69 Organisation for Economic Co-operation and Development. 2012. *Economic Policy Reforms 2012: Going for Growth.* OECD Publishing. https://doi.org/10.1787/growth-2012-en. | European Commission. 2013. The Growth Impact of Structural Reforms. *Quarterly Report on the Euro Area.* 12 (4). pp. 17–27. https://ec.europa.eu/economy_finance/publications/qr_euro_area/2013/pdf/qrea4_section_2_en.pdf. | International Monetary Fund. 2013b. *World Economic Outlook: Transitions and Tensions.* Washington, DC. October. https://www.imf.org/en/Publications/WEO/Issues/2016/12/31/Transitions-Tensions. | International Monetary Fund. 2016. Time for a Supply Side Boost? Macroeconomic Effects of Labor and Product Market Reforms in Advanced Economies. *World Economic Outlook: Too Slow for Too Long.* Chapter 3. Washington, DC. April. https://www.imf.org/en/Publications/WEO/Issues/2016/12/31/Too-Slow-for-Too-Long.

70 Meeting these objectives can strengthen aggregate demand by raising consumer and business confidence. They can promote medium-term economic prospects and living standards, by raising productivity and employment, and enhance the resilience of the economy to shocks. They can also affect inequality by changing the distribution of jobs and wages, and the allocation of income between labor and capital. | Footnote 11. | International Monetary Fund. 2019. Reigniting Growth in Low Income and Emerging Market Economies: What Role can Structural Reforms Play? *World Economic Outlook: Global Manufacturing Downturn, Rising Trade Barriers.* Chapter 3. Washington, DC. October. https://www.imf.org/en/Publications/WEO/Issues/2019/10/21/World-Economic-Outlook-October-2019-Global-Manufacturing-Downturn-Rising-Trade-Barriers-48513. | S. Aiyar et al. 2020. COVID-19: How Will European Banks Fare? *IMF Departmental Papers.* No. 2021/008. Washington, DC: International Monetary Fund. 26 March. https://www.imf.org/en/Publications/Departmental-Papers-Policy-Papers/Issues/2021/03/24/COVID-19-How-Will-European-Banks-Fare-50214.

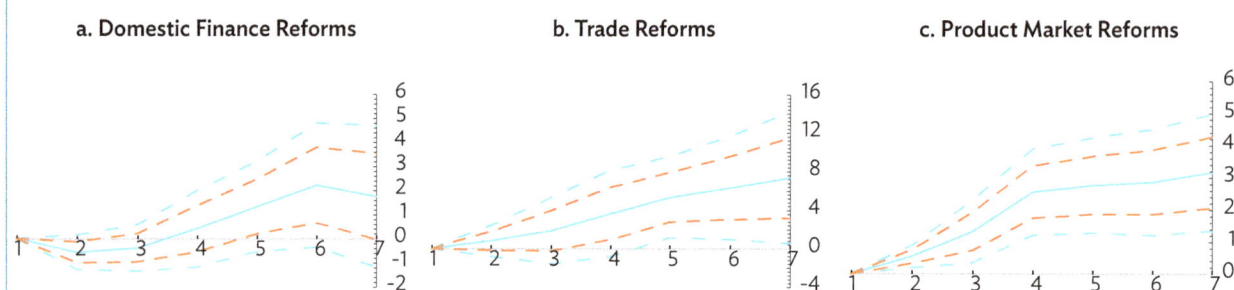

Figure 13: Average Macroeconomic Effects of (Selected) Structural Reforms on a Sample of Countries that Are Fragile and Conflict-Affected (As a Percentage of Real Gross Domestic Product)

a. Domestic Finance Reforms

b. Trade Reforms

c. Product Market Reforms

Notes:
1. The statistical method follows the approach proposed by Jordà (2005). The baseline specification controls for past economic growth and past reforms, as well as country and time-fixed effects.
2. The x-axis represents the years; t = 0 is the year of the shock; solid lines denote the response to a major historical reform; blue dashed lines denote 90% confidence bands; orange dashed lines denote 68% confidence bands, based on standard errors clustered at the country level.

Sources: Author's analysis based on
1. A. Alesina et al. 2020. Structural Reforms and Election: Evidence from a World-Wide New Dataset. *NBER Working Paper Series*. Working Paper No. 26720. National Bureau of Economic Research. January. https://www.nber.org/system/files/working_papers/w26720/w26720.pdf.;
2. For other macroeconomics variables: International Monetary Fund. Various years. World Economic Outlook databases. https://www.imf.org/en/Publications/SPROLLs/world-economic-outlook-databases#sort=%40imfdate%20descending;
3. O. Jordà. 2005. Estimation and Inference of Impulse Responses by Local Projections. *American Economic Review*. 95 (1). pp. 161–182. https://www.aeaweb.org/articles?id=10.1257/0002828053828518.

on earlier work from IMF (2019),[71] new empirical analysis shows that major historical reforms in a sample of fragile and conflicted-affected situations (FCAS) in the areas of domestic finance, trade, and product market have had sizable average positive effects on output over the medium term, reaching more than 2%, 8%, and 3%, respectively after 6 years (Figure 13). Product market deregulation pays off rather quickly in stimulating output. Overall, in normal times, the reforms analyzed do not appear to entail short-term macroeconomic costs.[72]

C. Aim for Budgetary Soundness by Focusing on Non-Oil Revenue with Tax Reforms[73]

On the fiscal front, tax reforms can be a driver for reshaping the social contract and accelerating development. A successful tax reform would aim at (i) increasing collection efficiency while minimizing distortions to economic activity; (ii) facilitating, accelerating, and professionalizing the interaction of the private sector with tax authorities; and (iii) establishing taxes gradually as a "fair" price for socioeconomic development.

When thinking about tax policy changes, one should bear in mind that the current discussion on the optimal tax structure is full of unsettled issues. The effects of the tax mix on long-term growth have been widely studied and the literature suggests that taxes are generally ranked from the most to the least detrimental to growth as follows:[74]

    (i)   corporate income tax (CIT);

---

71   Footnote 70 (2nd citation).
72   See Appendix 5 for technical details.
73   While any successful fiscal reform should be thought of in more general terms, that is, also considering the spending side of the budget and governance issues, this report aims to focus specifically on the revenue or taxation side and is, by no means, exhaustive.
74   For an extensive review of the literature on taxation and growth, see R. Kneller and F. Misch. 2011. What Does Ex-Post Evidence Tell Us About the Output Effects of Future Tax Reforms? ZEW– Centre for European Economic Research Discussion Paper No. 11-029. SSRN Electronic Journal. 1 April. https://papers.ssrn.com/sol3/papers.cfm?abstract_id=1810862. | J.M. Arnold et al. 2011. Tax Policy for Economic Recovery and Growth, *The Economic Journal*, 121 (550). pp. F59–F80. Oxford University Press. 1 February. https://doi.org/10.1111/j.1468-0297.2010.02415.x. | Footnote 46 (2nd citation).

(ii)   labor income taxes;

(iii) consumption taxes;[75]

(iv)   property taxes.

This said, the literature remains contentious: the ranking of instruments is not robust to different specifications,[76] and it implicitly assumes that tax design does not matter, which it manifestly does.

In general terms, a tax reform road map includes

(i)   broadening the tax base through limiting exemptions;

(ii)   simplifying tax systems;

(iii) enhancing the progressivity of personal income tax (PIT) (and raising rates where appropriate);

(iv)   on the tax and customs administration side, enhancing compliance and strengthening administrative capacity (which includes digital transformation of the tax administration); and

(v)   improving taxpayers' morale through enhanced transparency, improved access to information and taxpayer services, and better communication.

More broadly, it is important to provide a clear communication to assure taxpayers on the use of public funds, such as when part of the additional revenues is used to finance well-defined growth-enhancing capital spending and well-targeted social programs.

In addition to a revised tax procedure code mentioned earlier, one key reform Timor-Leste needs to consider is the introduction of value-added tax (VAT)—a form of indirect tax collected at various stages of production–distribution chains. If properly designed and implemented, the tax, at any stage, is effectively collected on the pure value added at that stage. The popularity of VAT comes from several sources, one being its potential scope for identifying and taxing the economic contribution made by any activity of a business of commercial nature.[77] The VAT has been adopted by more than 150 countries, in the majority of cases replacing distortionary cascading sales taxes and trade taxes. In fact, the introduction of VAT over the past few decades has been the most visible tax reform undertaken by developing countries,[78] leading to better revenues across the board.[79] Many developing countries have introduced the VAT to replace turnover tax or some type of single-stage sales tax.[80] The replaced taxes were inherently troublesome in terms of either revenue leakage or economic inefficiency or both.[81]

The VAT has several advantages. First, compared with alternatives in indirect taxation, the VAT has more revenue potential as it is generally more broad-based and entails a trail of invoices that helps improve tax compliance and enforcement. However, the compliance and administrative benefits can be overstated. The incentive to underreport

---

75   But if reform is aimed at removing VAT exemptions while lowering the marginal rate, consumption tax is beneficial. According to Gemmel (2014), consumption taxation is less harmful for growth than either personal or corporate taxation. | N. Gemmell, R. Kneller, and I. Sanz. 2013. The growth effects of tax rates in the OECD. *Canadian Journal of Economics*. 47, pp. 1217–1255. 1 March. https://papers.ssrn.com/sol3/papers.cfm?abstract_id=2256737. | S. Acosta Ormaechea and A. Morozumi. 2019. The Value Added Tax and Growth: Design Matters. IMF Working Papers. No. 2019/096. Washington, DC: *International Monetary Fund*. 7 May. https://www.imf.org/en/Publications/WP/Issues/2019/05/07/The-Value-Added-Tax-and-Growth-Design-Matters-46836.

76   J. Xing. 2012. Tax structure and growth: How robust is the empirical evidence? *Economics Letters* 117 (1). pp. 379–382. ScienceDirect, Elsevier. October. https://doi.org/10.1016/j.econlet.2012.05.054.

77   D. Williams. 1996. Value-Added Tax. In V. Thuronyi (ed). *Tax Law Design and Drafting*. International Monetary Fund. Washington, D.C. https://www.elibrary.imf.org/downloadpdf/book/9781557755872/9781557755872.pdf.

78   V. Tanzi, and H.H. Zee. 2000. Tax Policy for Emerging Markets: Developing Countries. *National Tax Journal*. 53 (2). pp. 299–322. University of Chicago Press. https://www.journals.uchicago.edu/doi/epdf/10.17310/ntj.2000.2.07.

79   M. Keen and B. Lockwood. 2010. The value added tax: Its causes and consequences. *Journal of Development Economics*. 92 (2). pp. 138-151. ScienceDirect, Elsevier. July. https://doi.org/10.1016/j.jdeveco.2009.01.012.

80   For example, the VAT, introduced in 1988 in the Philippines, replaced a web of indirect taxes including manufacturer's sales tax, turnover tax, advance sales tax on imports, miller's tax, forest charges, and other sorts of ad valorem taxes on services.

81   Opponents to the VAT usually argue that the VAT is more complex to administer than other types of consumption taxation, and the complexity naturally leads to higher collection costs. However, taxes replaced by the VAT in developing countries are generally far from being simple in their design and riddled with narrow base, multiple rates, and numerous exemptions.

VAT on output increases when sales are made to final consumers or to non-registered entities.[82] The possibility of claiming VAT refund also introduces a risk of fraudulent practices that other taxes that the VAT replaced do not suffer from. These risks can be important in Timor-Leste where a possible VAT implementation could coincide in the future with difficult budget situations, leading to the choice of high VAT rates, and too many exemptions. These, in turn, could shrink the tax base and break the VAT chain, weakening compliance and enforcement and providing more opportunities for fraudulent refund claims.

Second, invoice-based credit VAT, the most common form of VAT, is not only simple, but also, in principle, self-enforcing and hence a buoyant tax.[83] Being a buoyant tax, the VAT may allow for some relief in income taxes; and if the VAT introduction accompanies a reduction in income taxes, the whole tax system tends to be politically more acceptable and, hence, more stable. Relatedly, there is also the issue of it being economically neutral and a powerful tool for economic stabilization,[84] which is pertinent for Timor-Leste.

Third, unlike income taxes, consumption-based VAT does not distort consumption–savings–investment decision. In other words, it targets a large tax base and figures among the least growth-damaging taxes. In practice, however, this quality depends largely on the design features of the VAT such as the number of rates, the prevalence of exemptions, the level and number of registration thresholds, and the limitations on refunding excess VAT credit, just to name a few.[85] While the production-neutrality property of the VAT has generally been an important factor in the decision to adopt it, the benefits from such neutrality—in terms of improving resource allocation in an economy—are usually less important in developing countries, such as Timor-Leste, where the number of production stages is relatively small since typically, they rely heavily on agricultural activities. The box provides a succinct discussion of successful country stories related to the introduction of VAT.

Box: Case Studies on Value-Added Tax Reforms

Bangladesh (2006–2013)

Deep reform of the tax system took place in 1991 when the government introduced the value-added tax (VAT). However, even this reform came about painfully, with implementation put off long enough for all the country's organized special interests to conspire within the political system to ensure that the VAT would be riddled with protections, exemptions, and weak sanctions. At the insistence of the International Monetary Fund (IMF), the government agreed to prepare a new VAT law to address weaknesses in the 1991 law. It took until 2013 to enact a new VAT law.

Outcome: The tax ratio rose from 7.5% of gross domestic product (GDP) in 2006 to 9.7% in 2013, a 30% increase. While some of this increased revenue resulted from an increase in VAT revenue by about 0.7 percentage points of GDP, the bigger increase came from income taxes.

continued on next page

---

82 The credit-invoice mechanism may even create informality chains as stressed by de Paula and Scheinkman (2010) in Brazil. | A. de Paula and J.A. Scheinkman. 2009. The Informal Sector: An Equilibrium Model and Some Empirical Evidence from Brazil. *The Review of Income and Wealth.* 57(s1). pp. S8–S26. Wiley. 9 May. https://onlinelibrary.wiley.com/doi/epdf/10.1111/j.1475-4991.2011.00450.x.

83 L. de Mello. 2008. Avoiding the Value-added Tax: Theory and Cross-country Evidence. *Public Finance Review.* 37(1). pp. 27–46. Sage Publications. 6 May. https://journals.sagepub.com/doi/abs/10.1177/1091142108316588. | A. A. Tait. 1991. *Value-Added Tax: International Practice and Problems.* (Second reprint). Washington, DC: International Monetary Fund. | Ebrill, Keen, and Perry (2001) shows that this was true for all regions, except for Central Europe, the Russian Federation, and some other countries of the former Soviet Union. | L.P. Ebrill, M. Keen and V.J. Perry. 2001. *The Modern VAT.* Washington, DC: International Monetary Fund.

84 R.W. Lindholm. 1970. The Value Added Tax: A Short Review of the Literature. *Journal of Economic Literature.* 8 (4). pp. 1178–1189. American Economic Association. December. https://ideas.repec.org/a/aea/jeclit/v8y1970i4p1178-89.html.

85 R. Bird and P. P. Gendron. 2011. *The VAT in Developing and Transitional Countries.* Cambridge University Press. https://doi.org/10.1017/CBO9780511619366.

Afghanistan (2003–2012)

Starting in 2003 and 2004, Afghanistan launched measures to build the domestic tax system. These included introducing a number of simplified taxes, including a turnover tax called the Business Receipts Tax (BRT) and withholding on wages. In 2009, Afghanistan drafted a new VAT law to progressively replace the BRT through the lowering of the VAT registration threshold over time. The VAT law was enacted in the first quarter of 2015 with a start date of December 2016.

Outcome: Given the low base that it started from, Afghanistan has been quite successful in its efforts to establish a more modern tax system. Tax offices are open around the country, the number of active taxpayers has increased, normal income taxes have been established, and tax revenue rose drastically from 2.5% of GDP in 2003 to 8.0% in 2012.

Georgia (2005–2009)

Between 2004 and 2009, tax reforms focused on simplifying the tax code and lowering tax rates. The VAT rate was brought down from 20% to 18%. The State Revenue Service strengthened tax collection by streamlining and automating most processes, introducing risk-based audit management and vastly expanding e-services. This simplified taxpayer requirements and greatly reduced face-to-face time between tax officers and taxpayers.

Outcome: Georgia's tax revenues have increased more than fourfold thanks to the combined effect of the changes in the tax regulation and administration. Revenues from VAT rose from 8.5% of GDP in 2005 to 11.3% in 2009.

Ghana (1995–1998)

The VAT, first introduced in Ghana in March 1995, was intended to overcome problems in the existing sales tax system—narrow base, weak administration, and corruption-prone physical surveillance. The VAT rate was set at 17.5%, higher than the rate of 15% applied in the replaced sales tax. A new revenue collection agency, the VAT Service, was established. A computer system was developed. However, the VAT was removed within 4 months of its introduction. The failure was due to multiple problems rooted in the tax policy design, timing, and implementation.

The VAT was reintroduced in 1998. Some key factors for the success of the 1998 introduction of VAT:

(i)   strong, clear political commitment from government leaders;
(ii)   good preparation for the tax administration;
(iii)   reasonably low introductory rate, high registration threshold, and good timing for the VAT introduction; and
(iv)   well-designed public education campaign.

Trinidad and Tobago (1983–1989)

Tax reform in Trinidad and Tobago was comprehensive, covering both direct and indirect taxes. The VAT was introduced in 1989 when income from oil started falling to replace the previous purchase tax (which exposed a number of problems). However, the VAT legislation was not enacted until September 1989. Multiple other taxes were eliminated (e.g., purchase taxes; consolidated special levy; electricity and telephone taxes; hotel room tax; domestic stamp duties). The introduction of the VAT was assessed as successful. In the 1991 budget, the tax was expected to yield 25% of the total revenue, whereas the replaced purchase tax contributed just less than 9%.

continued on next page

Box: continued

Some key lessons for the success are as follows:
  (i)   strong political commitment;
  (ii)   careful planning at all stages, from designing to administration;
  (iii)   low introductory rate;
  (iv)   close cooperation between businesses and government;
  (v)   public and taxpayers' education;
  (vi)   combination with abolishment of purchase taxes and reduction of income tax rates;
  (vii)   selection of capable staff for the administration;
  (viii)   good timing for the VAT introduction.

Sources:
1.   E. Chapman. 2001. Introducing a Value Added Tax: Lessons from Ghana. PREM Notes. No. 61. Washington, DC: World Bank. December. https://openknowledge.worldbank.org/handle/10986/11360
2.   J.F. Due and F.P. Greaney. 1992. The Introduction of a Value-Added Tax in Trinidad and Tobago. In R.M. Bird and M. Casanegra de Jantscher, eds. Improving Tax Administration in Developing Countries. Chapter 5. Washington, DC: International Monetary Fund. https://doi.org/10.5089/9781557753175.071.
3.   Ernst & Young LLP. 1995. VAT & Sales Taxes Worldwide: A Guide to Practice and Procedures in 61 Countries. New York: John Wiley & Sons.
4.   PricewaterhouseCoopers LLP. 2002. Corporate Taxes 2002-2003: Worldwide Summaries. New Jersey: John Wiley & Sons
5.   Organisation for Economic Co-operation and Development. 2015. Examples of Successful DRM Reforms and the Role of International Co-operation, Discussion Paper, OECD Publishing. July. https://www.oecd.org/ctp/tax-global/examples-of-successful-DRM-reforms-and-the-role-of-international-co-operation.pdf.

The precise impact of new reform measures, such as a VAT introduction, is difficult to quantify owing to possible cyclical factors playing a role. That said, back-of-the-envelope calculations for Timor-Leste can be done using private consumption expenditure as the relevant tax base proxy[86] and assuming alternative standard VAT rates.[87] In addition, one as to consider the existence of VAT gaps—the difference between the VAT due and the actual VAT revenues—since in most countries, including advanced ones, this gap is rarely zero.

The underlying reasons for the VAT gap can be grouped into four broad categories: (i) VAT fraud and VAT evasion; (ii) VAT avoidance practices and optimization; (iii) bankruptcies and financial insolvencies; and (iv) administrative errors. For reference, an interval based on EU evidence is constructed: the smallest VAT gaps were observed in Croatia (1%), Sweden (1.4%), and Cyprus (2.7%); the largest in Romania (34.9%), Greece (25.8%), and Malta (23.5%).[88] Some calculations yield a range of VAT collection (accounting for plausible VAT gaps) between 4.5% and 10.2% on non-oil gross domestic product (GDP) in 2020. Since the 2020 value for tax revenue was 7.5% of non-oil GDP, the introduction of the VAT would, at the minimum (with a 10% standard rate and about 35% of VAT gap), account for close to 60% the current level of tax revenues (Figure 14).

---

86   In fact, apropos the World Bank's World Development Indicators (2020), the variable relied upon for Timor-Leste is final consumption expenditure of households and nonprofit institutions serving households (NPISH). It represents the market value of all goods and services, including durable products (such as cars, washing machines, and home computers), purchased by households. It excludes purchases of dwellings but includes imputed rent for owner-occupied dwellings. It also includes payments and fees to governments to obtain permits and licenses.
87   Ebrill et al. (2001) survey shows that the VAT performs relatively well in small countries and islands. | Footnote 83 (3rd citation).
88   G. Poniatowski, M. Bonch-Osmolovskiy, and A. Śmietanka. 2021. VAT gap in the EU: Report 2021, European Commission, Directorate-General for Taxation and Customs Union, Publications Office. https://data.europa.eu/doi/10.2778/447556.

Figure 14: Value-Added Tax Revenue Collection Assuming Different Standard Rates

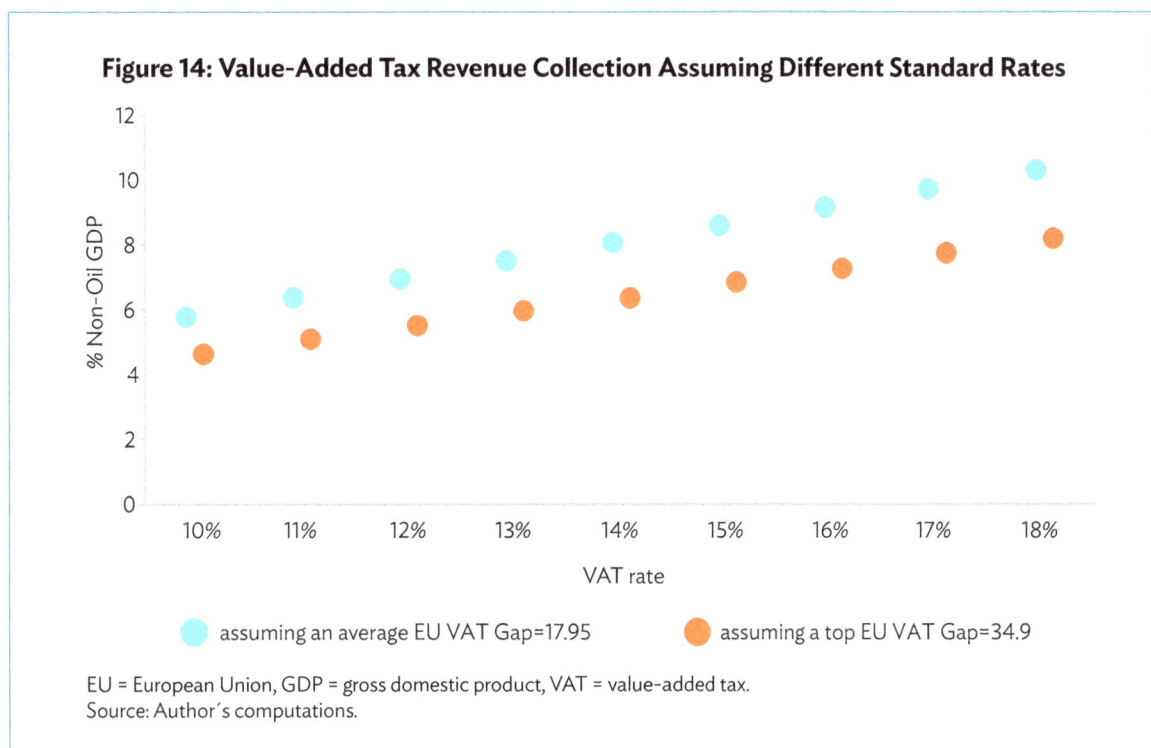

assuming an average EU VAT Gap=17.95   assuming a top EU VAT Gap=34.9

EU = European Union, GDP = gross domestic product, VAT = value-added tax.
Source: Author's computations.

Finally, related to the need to change and diversify the economic structure, several studies find a negative influence from the agriculture share of GDP; the use of multiple and complex taxes; and exemptions on the decision to adopt a VAT and its revenue collection impact.[89] Moreover, indirect taxes (including the VAT) are likely to perform better in countries which rely more on foreign trade. Prest (1979) further argues that the overall tax capacity of a country is positively correlated with the size of trade.[90] This relates to section IV.A on diversifying the economy toward more tradable sectors with higher value-added content.

D. Be Mindful of the Distributional Effects of Tax Reforms and Their Political Viability

Conventionally, a tax system is considered to be regressive if the share of tax burden in total income is reduced as income rises. Defined this way, regressivity is inherently applied to the VAT, a tax on consumption: poor people generally spend a greater portion of their income on consumption than rich people. But while VAT can be designed to be a "money machine" and allow developing countries to raise revenues efficiently (with the least collection cost), it does not have equity as a primary objective. For this reason, the distributional impact of the VAT should not be analyzed in isolation, but in a broader context of the whole fiscal system encompassing both tax and expenditure programs. Progressivity is best achieved by complementing the VAT with a functioning income tax system, selective excises, and prudent, pro-poor expenditures. However, in poor developing countries such as Timor-Leste, the base of the PIT is typically narrow and tax administrations do not have sufficient capacity to collect the tax properly. It is, therefore, critically important to maintain a buoyant VAT system to efficiently collect revenues, which are, in turn, channeled to help poor people through pro-poor social programs such as housing, health care, and education. That said, countries

---

89   For sub-Saharan Africa, see T. Addison and J. Levin. 2012. The determinants of tax revenue in sub-Saharan Africa. https://www.semanticscholar.org/paper/The-determinants-of-tax-revenue-in-sub-Saharan-Addison-Levin/84e0fb345d98749b880a559a 39ff8559cab96723 | For Poland, see A. Kaczynska. 2015. The analysis of VAT revenue in Poland: The size and determinants. The 3rd Global Virtual Conference, 6–10 April. | For 143 countries, see Footnote 79.
90   A.R. Prest. 1979. The Taxable Capacity of a Country. In J.F.J. Toye, ed. *Taxation and Economic Development*. Chapter 1. London: Frank Cass.

with a VAT commonly attempt to incorporate in it various progressivity features with multiple exemptions, zero rates, and reduced rates for the goods or services consumed mostly by poor people.[91]

Since any policy change can have both economic and distributional effects, making fundamental transformations to a tax structure of any country—Timor-Leste included—is politically challenging. Resistance from vested interests can impede the implementation of measures with revenue potential.[92] This is likely to be the case with attempts to make the tax system more progressive as opposition from richer people will surface. The resistance to tax reforms is channeled through the prevailing political system. In Timor-Leste, the Fiscal Reform Commission created in 2016 to design and implement a comprehensive reform program was unfortunately decommissioned in 2019. Moreover, little of the planned legislation proposed by the government was enacted.

In a recent paper, Gupta and Jalles (2020) studied the experience of tax reforms in 45 emerging and low-income countries. They found that left-wing governments are less inclined to implement tax changes, while both proximity to elections and political strength or cohesion are positively associated with tax reforms.[93] It seems that left-leaning governments are distrustful of modifications to tax systems presumably because they view them as favoring rich people. A reform of trade taxes is also not favored as it exposes small businesses to greater international competition with implications for employment. Interestingly, revenue administration reforms are resisted the most by left-leaning governments. Proximity to elections seems to trigger reforms of PIT but the opposite holds true for trade tax reforms.

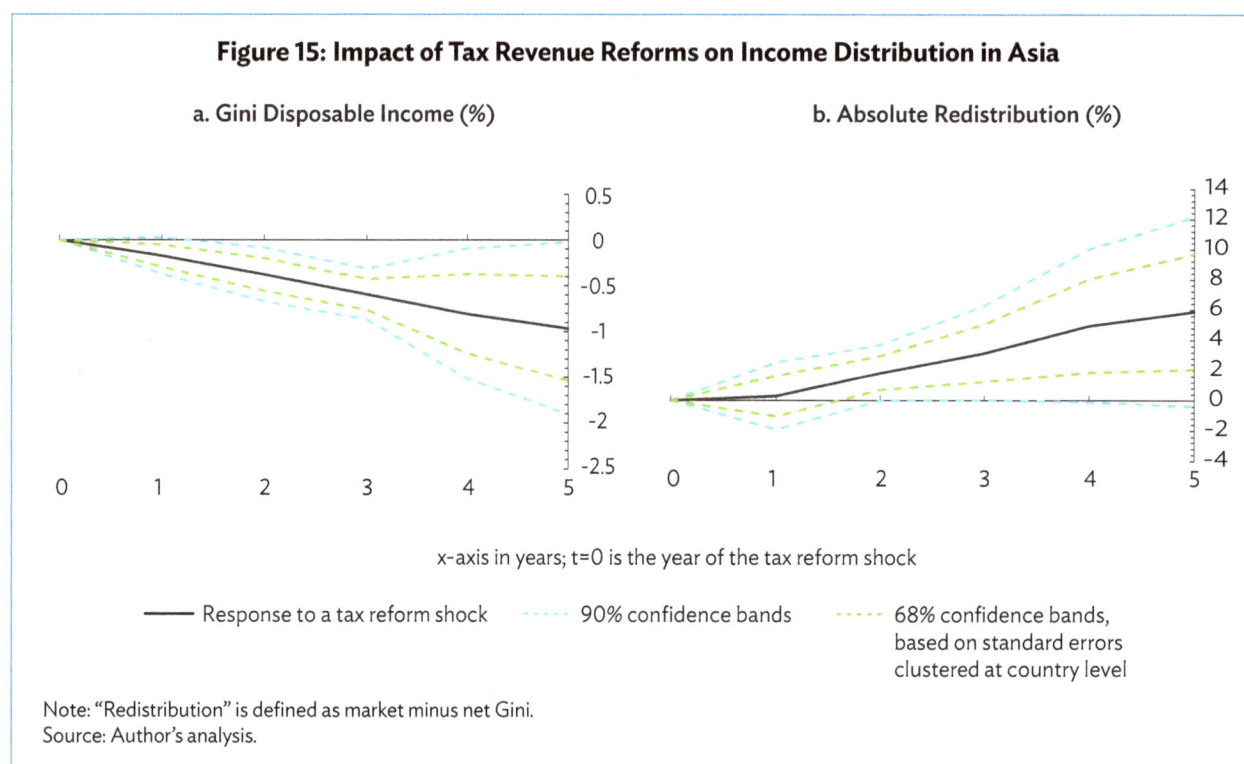

Figure 15: Impact of Tax Revenue Reforms on Income Distribution in Asia

a. Gini Disposable Income (%)

b. Absolute Redistribution (%)

x-axis in years; t=0 is the year of the tax reform shock

—— Response to a tax reform shock   ----- 90% confidence bands   ----- 68% confidence bands, based on standard errors clustered at country level

Note: "Redistribution" is defined as market minus net Gini.
Source: Author's analysis.

---

91   Tait (1991) indicates that in the UK, zero-rating food and other basic goods consumed by poor people made the VAT even progressive. Trinidad and Tobago also incorporated in its VAT regime numerous zero rates and exemptions that were intended to make the system less regressive than the replaced purchase tax. | Footnote 83 (2nd citation).
92   Footnote 12.
93   S. Gupta and J.T. Jalles. 2020. On the Political Economy Determinants of Tax Reforms: Evidence from Developing Countries. CGD Policy Paper 199. Washington, DC: Center for Global Development. 15 December. https://www.cgdev.org/sites/default/files/PP199-Gupta-Jalles-Political-Economy-Full.pdf.

That said, certain types of tax reforms can engender political support in their favor since they can be equity-enhancing.[94] This has been the case for reforms in PIT and tax administration. A new analysis conducted for this report for a sample of eight countries in developing Asia (not including Timor-Leste) that implemented tax reforms in these two areas between 2000 and 2015 shows that, indeed, they have been equity enhancing.[95] Figure 15 shows a decline in disposable-income Gini index following a tax reform in year t=0 while at the same time, the degree of the tax-benefit system redistribution goes up.

---

94 Footnote 55.
95 Developing Asian countries included are: Cambodia, the Lao PDR, Maldives, Nepal, the Philippines, Solomon Islands, Tonga, and Tuvalu. See Appendix 6 for technical details.

V CONCLUSION AND POLICY SUGGESTIONS

Timor-Leste has substantially improved its revenue performance since 2000. However, the COVID-19 pandemic crisis has both increased spending and reduced tax receipts. Once the pandemic is over, putting the fiscal position on a more solid ground should be a priority. But such fiscal consolidation should measure the trade-off between magnitude and length so that is minimizes the effect of growth (and developmental needs).

From the analysis conducted, it can be concluded that fiscal policy in Timor-Leste has not been stabilizing macroeconomic fluctuations over the last couple of decades—which is one of its key functions.[96] Automatic stabilizers are absent and they need to be reinforced to increase resilience to future shocks. In comparison with other similar countries in the region and outside, Timor-Leste collects relatively little non-oil tax revenue. This is at odds with the large public expenditure envelope (and enlarging deficits) which basically survives thanks to withdrawals from the Petroleum Fund (which, according to recent IMF estimates, is depleting at a fast rate). Moreover, Timor-Leste's tax system is characterized by low tax collection and low tax effort. At the same time, while Timor-Leste's tax system displays statistically significant long-run buoyancy of higher than 1 (suggestive that growth has improved fiscal sustainability over time), as it stands, it is neither good nor bad as an automatic stabilizer. Looking specifically at some of its tax policy instruments, Timor-Leste occupies the worst position out of countries in developing Asia that have CIT productivity data available.

Against this background, it is important that Timor-Leste's productive structure moves away from non-tradables toward higher valued-added tradable sectors. This will accomplish multiple objectives: (i) reduce vulnerability to climate shocks as the country becomes less dependent on agriculture; (ii) provide incentives to increase formality and hence bring more people and businesses into the tax net; and (iii) propel growth (whose positive externality is to bring in additional revenue due to increased activity, and reduce poverty and inequality). Since the trend growth observed in earlier years is unlikely to be sustained, the government needs to embark on comprehensive reforms to mobilize more domestic resources. Building fiscal systems in fragile contexts, such as in Timor-Leste, should start with the basics. Simply getting taxpayers into the tax net can yield important gains. This means reorganizing the tax administration to streamline operations, strengthening compliance management and, at the same time, improving responsiveness to taxpayer needs. Achieving sustainable improvements in revenues requires a balanced approach to compliance improvement. In most success cases, host country authorities and their development partners have embraced a dual strategy of supporting voluntary compliance on the one hand, while pursuing noncompliant taxpayers through enhanced enforcement on the other.

Tax policy reforms have been shown to be important to support domestic revenue (or resource) mobilization (DRM) efforts. The introduction of a modern value-added tax (VAT), in particular, can complement other tax administration reforms. As mentioned in the different case studies identified earlier, introducing a modern VAT to replace archaic, cumbersome, and distorting taxes on company sales or turnover is typically a good policy decision. In each of those cases, the VAT brought in greater revenue than the taxes it replaced and arguably at lower growth costs. Since the VAT proves to be an efficient tool for revenue collection, its performance, therefore, has direct impact on fiscal mobilization, macroeconomic stability, and development. In the case of Timor-Leste, the introduction of the VAT would, at the minimum (with a 10% standard rate and about 35 % of VAT gap), account for close to 60% the current level of tax revenues.

---

96   R.A. Musgrave. 1959. *The Theory of Public Finance: A Study in Public Economy*. McGraw-Hill.

In this regard, a golden rule in designing an efficient VAT is that the tax be imposed on pure consumption, broad-based, and comprehensive in coverage over the whole production–distribution chain. The common form of VAT is consumption-type and applied on destination principle with invoice-based credit method. The practical advice is that the VAT rate structure should be designed as simply as possible, preferably with one or—at most—two positive rates, few exemptions, and zero rating being exclusively granted to exports. If so designed, the VAT is buoyant and efficient as one would desire for Timor-Leste.[97]

Assuming this is the direction the government would like to pursue, distributional consequences would have to be factored in, particularly since the VAT is inherently regressive. Many countries, to reduce regressivity, do one or several of the following: exempting, zero rating, or excluding certain essential consumption goods from the tax base (e.g., foodstuff, medicine, health care). Giving preferential treatment to particular goods, however, is an inefficient way to make the tax less regressive because high-income households consume more of the goods in question (though less as a share of income) than low-income households do. A better approach is to provide limited cash payment—that is, a refundable tax credit. That way, everyone receives the same benefit, in dollars, which translates into a larger share of low-income households' income.[98] This said, it is critical that regressivity be studied in an overall context of the applicable fiscal policies. In designing its reform program, Timor-Leste's government should bear in mind that some reforms mentioned might yield highly uneven gains across the population.[99] In this regard, the government may need to overcome the political opposition to reforms from different pressure groups. The country's policymakers should factor in and implement up-front complementary reforms by enhancing redistribution through the tax-benefit system. Otherwise, reforms whose gains are captured only by a small fraction of society risk losing support and stalling, or being undone, down the road.[100]

Finally, greater mobilization of domestic resources should go together with improving efficiency of public spending (which is beyond the scope of this report).[101] There is no point in collecting more taxes domestically if they are used to finance inefficient programs.[102] Increased spending allocations and better targeting of social spending would help offset some of the regressivity stemming from indirect taxes.

---

97 Broadening base, in general sense, reduces deadweight loss and provides an opportunity for lowering the rates, and, thereby, increasing compliance. Note that zero-rating generally provides strong incentives for frauds, creates excessive burden on tax administration, and effectively erodes the base.

98 E. Toder, J. Nunns, and J. Rosenberg. 2012. Implications of Different Bases for a VAT. Washington, DC: Urban-Brookings Tax Policy Center. https://www.urban.org/sites/default/files/publication/25086/412501-Implications-of-Different-Bases-for-a-VAT.PDF.

99 K. R. Fabrizio, S. Poczter, and B. A. Zelner. 2017. Does innovation policy attract international competition? Evidence from energy storage. *Research Policy*. 46 (6). pp. 1106–1117. ScienceDirect, Elsevier. July. https://www.sciencedirect.com/science/article/abs/pii/S0048733317300665. | D. Furceri, P. Loungani, and J. D. Ostry. 2018. The Aggregate and Distributional Effects of Financial Globalization: Evidence from Macro and Sectoral Data. *IMF Working Papers*. Paper No. 2018/083. 6 April. https://www.imf.org/en/Publications/WP/Issues/2018/04/11/The-Aggregate-and-Distributional-Effects-of-Financial-Globalization-Evidence-from-Macro-and-45772.

100 A. Alesina et al. 2020. Structural Reforms and Election: Evidence from a World-Wide New Dataset. NBER Working Paper Series. Working Paper No. 26720. National Bureau of Economic Research. January. https://www.nber.org/system/files/working_papers/w26720/w26720.pdf.

101 Footnote 53.

102 S. Gupta. 2018. Merely Collecting More Taxes Is Not Enough to Achieve the SDGs. Center for Global Development. 17 July. https://www.cgdev.org/blog/merely-collecting-more-taxes-not-enough-achieve-sdgs#:~:text=In%20development%20circles%20these%20days%2C%20there%20is%20considerable,the%20SDGs%20if%20the%20revenues%20are%20spent%20efficiently.

APPENDIX 1
COMPUTING POTENTIAL GROSS DOMESTIC PRODUCT: APPLICATION TO TIMOR-LESTE

Despite substantial progress in the estimation methodologies to calculate potential output, there is still not a widely accepted approach in the profession.[1] The estimation methods that are currently used by national and international institutions are built on one of the following principles (or some combination thereof).[2]

Principle 1. Potential output is simply estimated as trend output through the application of statistical univariate filters to the series of actual output, which consists of filtering out the trend component from the cyclical one.

Alternatively, there are structural approaches, which derive the estimates directly from the theoretical structure of a model.

Principle 2. Non-Accelerating Inflation Rate of Unemployment is estimated by using inflation data, usually by means of a Phillips curve, on the theoretical principle that positive (negative) inflation changes must correspond to negative (positive) unemployment gaps, and then output gaps are computed on the basis of such unemployment gaps.

Principle 3. By means of an explicit model of the economy, estimates may be drawn directly from the evolution of supply factors over time, on the theoretical principle that growth of potential output is exclusively a supply-side phenomenon. This class of models includes the production function approach, which obtains potential output by applying an aggregate production function to the time series of estimated potential inputs and potential total factor productivity. The majority of estimation models of the main international institutions are based nowadays on such a method.[3]

---

1   C. Borio, P. Disyatat, and M. Juselius. 2013. Rethinking Potential Output: Embedding Information about the Financial Cycle. *BIS Working Papers*. No. 404. Monetary and Economic Department, Bank of International Settlements. February. https://www.bis.org/publ/work404.pdf. | C. Borio, P. Disyatat, and M. Juselius. 2014. A Parsimonious Approach to Incorporating Economic Information in Measures of Potential Output. *BIS Working Papers*. No. 442. Monetary and Economic Department, Bank of International Settlements. February. https://www.bis.org/publ/work442.pdf.

2   For surveys on potential output estimation methods see, for example, D. Ladiray, G. L. Mazzi, and F. Sartori. 2003. Statistical Methods for Potential Output Estimation and Cycle Extraction. Luxembourg: Office for Official Publications of the European Communities. https://ec.europa.eu/eurostat/documents/3888793/5815765/KS-AN-03-015-EN.PDF.pdf/19128aef-fe5c-47ea-b7a1-c1f6a412258e?t=1414778813000. | G. Horn, C. Logeay, and S. Tober. 2007. Methodological Issues of Medium-Term Macroeconomic Projections: The Case of Potential Output. No. 04-2007. IMK Studies. IMK at the Hans Boeckler Foundation, Macroeconomic Policy Institute. https://EconPapers.repec.org/RePEc:imk:studie:04-2007. | A. Bassanetti, M. Caivano, and A. Locarno. 2010. Modelling Italian Potential Output and the Output Gap. Bank of Italy Temi di Discussione (Working Paper) No. 771. 10 September. http://dx.doi.org/10.2139/ssrn.1788071. | R. Anderton et al. 2014. Potential output from a euro area perspective. *Occasional Paper Series*. No. 156. Frankfurt: European Central Bank. November. https://op.europa.eu/en/publication-detail/-/publication/9e45aedd-ad92-455f-a2af-ef3fd01c355b/language-en. | A. Alichi et al. 2017. Multivariate Filter Estimation of Potential Output for the United States. *IMF Working Papers*. No. 2017/106. Washington, DC: International Monetary Fund. 4 May. https://www.imf.org/en/Publications/WP/Issues/2017/05/04/Multivariate-Filter-Estimation-of-Potential-Output-for-the-United-States-44882.

3   Other methods in this class are those based on structural systems of simultaneous equations. These include the structural VAR models (sVARs), in which all variables are regarded as endogenous and the economy can be affected by more than one type of disturbance (O.J. Blanchard and D. Quah. 1989. The Dynamic Effects of Aggregate Supply and Demand Disturbances. *American Economic Review*. 79 (4). pp. 655–673. American Economic Association. September. http://www.jstor.org/stable/1827924. | Footnote 2 of Appendix 1 (2nd citation), and the dynamic stochastic general equilibrium (DSGE) (I. Vetlov et al. 2011. Potential output in DSGE model. ECB Working Paper. No. 1351. Frankfurt: European Central Bank. https://www.econstor.eu/bitstream/10419/153785/1/ecbwp1351.pdf). | The former identifies different types of shocks and assumes that only structural shocks affect potential. The latter estimates potential output by calibrating a DSGE model on the economy then simulating a path without demand disturbances. In both cases, the high number of unknown parameters and the difficult identification of the nature of disturbances imply many arbitrary assumptions and high sensitivity of the estimates to model specification. | Footnote 2 of Appendix 1 (5th citation).

In what follows, attention is focused first on univariate statistical methods. Note, however, that statistical methods are anything but "theory-free" (as they are sometimes defined),[4] being instead based on the purely theoretical presumption that actual output tends to fluctuate around potential output. In this class of methods, actual output is prevented by construction from deviating other than temporarily from potential output, with the greater or lesser adherence between the two series entirely depending on the statistical definition of cycle and trend.

Mindful of the criticisms surrounding the use of the popular Hodrick–Prescott (HP) (1981)[5] filter (such as the identification of spurious cycles),[6] the recent filtering technique developed by Hamilton (2018) is applied for the purpose of this study.[7]

To extract the cyclical and trend components for a generic variable x_t (denoted x_t^c and x_t^τ, respectively) where in our case $x_t = \{GDP_t\}$, we begin by employing the commonly used HP filter. This filter minimizes the following function:

$$\min_{\tau_t}\left\{\sum_{t=1}^{T}(x_t - x_t^\tau)^2 + \lambda\sum_{t=1}^{T}[(x_t^\tau - x_{t-1}^\tau) - (x_{t-1}^\tau - x_{t-2}^\tau)]^2\right\} \qquad \text{(A1)}$$

where λ is the smoothing parameter. The greater the value of λ, the larger is the penalty on variations of the trend's growth rate (i.e., the sum of the squares of the trend's second differences). Hodrick and Prescott suggest 100 or 1,600 as a value for λ for annual or quarterly data, respectively.

We then compare the obtained HP-based cyclical and trend components with the ones stemming out of applying Hamilton's (2018)—arguably better—filtering method. Hamilton (2018) presents evidence against using the HP filter. He writes that:

(i) "The HP filter produces series with spurious dynamic relations that have no basis in the underlying data-generating process.

(ii) A one-sided version of the filter reduces but does not eliminate spurious predictability and, moreover, produces series that do not have the properties sought by most potential users of the HP filter.

(iii) A statistical formalization of the problem typically produces values for the smoothing parameter vastly at odds with common practice, e.g., a value for λ far below 1,600 for quarterly data.

(iv) There's a better alternative. A regression of the variable at date t+h on the four most recent values as of date t offers a robust approach to detrending that achieves all the objectives sought by users of the HP filter with none of its drawbacks."

For that purpose, we estimate:

$$x_{t+h} = \gamma_0 + \sum_{j=0}^{k}\gamma_j + x_{t-j} + u_{t+h} \qquad \text{(A2)}$$

where $x_t = x_t^\tau + x_t^c$. The non-stationary part of the regression provides the cyclical component:

---

4   Footnote 2 of Appendix 1 (3rd citation).
5   R. J. Hodrick and E. C. Prescott. 1981. Post-war U.S. Business Cycles: An Empirical Investigation. Discussion Paper 451. Center for Mathematical Studies in Economics and Management Science, Northwestern University. May. https://www.kellogg.northwestern.edu/research/math/papers/451.pdf.
6   A. C. Harvey and A. Jaeger. 1993. Detrending, stylized facts and the business cycle. *Journal of Applied Econometrics*. 8 (3). pp. 231-47. Wiley. July–September. https://doi.org/10.1002/jae.3950080302. | T. Cogley and J. M. Nason. 1995. Effects of the Hodrick-Prescott filter on trend and difference stationary time series: Implications for business cycle research. *Journal of Economic Dynamics and Control*. 19 (1-2). pp. 253–78. ScienceDirect, Elsevier. Januray–February. https://doi.org/10.1016/0165-1889(93)00781-X.
7   J. D. Hamilton. 2018. Why you should never use the Hodrick-Prescott filter. *The Review of Economics and Statistics*. 100 (5). pp. 831–843. MIT Press Direct. December. https://doi.org/10.1162/rest_a_00706.

$$x_t^c = \hat{u}_t \qquad \text{(A3)}$$

while the trend is given by

$$x_t^\tau = \hat{\gamma}_0 + \sum_{j=0}^{k} \hat{\gamma}_j + x_{t-h-j} \qquad \text{(A4)}$$

Hamilton (2018) suggests that h and k should be chosen such that the residuals from equation (A3) are stationary and points out that, for a broad array of processes, the fourth differences of a series are indeed stationary. We choose h = 2 and k = 3, which is line with the dynamics seen in gross domestic product (GDP). Equations (A2), (A3), and (A4) are estimated using ordinary least squares (OLS).

Hodrick (2020) subsequently examined whether the proposed alternative approach of Hamilton (2018) was actually better than the HP filter at extracting the cyclical component of several simulated time series calibrated to approximate real GDP of the United States. Hodrick (2020) finds that for time series in which there are distinct growth and cyclical components, the HP filter comes closer to isolating the cyclical component than the Hamilton alternative.

Finally, we also use the Baxter–King (1999)[8] (BK) and Christiano–Fitzgerald (2003)[9] (CF) band-pass filters. Baxter and King derive a finite approximation to the infinite-order symmetric moving-average filter by estimating the cyclical component of a time series as:

$$x_t^c = \sum_{j=-k}^{k} \hat{\gamma}_j x_{t-j} \qquad \text{(A5)}$$

where $\hat{\gamma}_j$ are the modified weights for a finite-order symmetric moving-average filter such that $\sum_{j=-k}^{k} \hat{\gamma}_i = 0$, $\hat{\gamma}_j = \gamma_j - \overline{\gamma}_k$ and $\hat{\gamma}_j = \gamma_{-j}$ with γ_j being the ideal weight in the time domain and $\overline{\gamma}_k$, its mean truncated at ±k. Removing the cyclical component of the time series x_t provides the trend component x_t^T. Similarly, CF derives a finite approximation to the ideal band-pass filter by minimizing the mean squared error between the filtered series and the series filtered by an ideal band-pass filter, with the cyclical component given by:

$$x_t^c = \gamma_0 x_t + \sum_{j=1}^{T-t-1} \gamma_j x_{t+j} + \overline{\gamma}_{T-t} x_T + \sum_{j=1}^{t-2} \gamma_j x_{t-j} + \overline{\gamma}_{t-1} x_1 \qquad \text{(A6)}$$

where $\gamma_0, \gamma_1, \dots$ are the weights used by the ideal band-pass filter and $\overline{\gamma}_{T-t}$ and $\overline{\gamma}_{t-1}$ are linear functions of the ideal weights.

In what follows, data at annual frequency from IMF's World Economic Outlook database is used. Table 1A shows the bivariate correlations between cyclical and trend components by type of filtering technique using the IMF real GDP for Timor-Leste. The BK cycles are highly correlated with that from the HP filter, while CF cycles are less so. The correlation of the Hamilton cycle with that from other filters is similar and above 50% except with BK and CF. Turning to the structural (or trend) components, irrespectively of the filter, they are all similarly highly correlated amongst each other. Figure 1A compares the cyclical and trend components of the four filters together.

---

8   M. Baxter and R. King. 1995. Measuring Business Cycles: Approximate Band-Pass Filters for Economic Time Series. *NBER Working Paper Series*. Working Paper No. 5022. Cambridge, Massachusetts: National Bureau of Economic Research. February. https://www.nber.org/system/files/working_papers/w5022/w5022.pdf.

9   L. Christiano and T. Fitzgerald. 2003. The Band Pass Filter. *International Economic Review*. 44 (2). pp. 435–465. Wiley-Blackwell. May. https://doi.org/10.1111/1468-2354.t01-1-00076.

Table 1A: Correlations between Cyclical and Trend Components of Gross Domestic Product by Filter, Timor-Leste, 2002–2020

Cyclical Component	HP (100)	BK	CF	Hamilton
HP (100)	1			
BK	0.91	1		
CF	0.76	0.89	1	
Hamilton	0.53	0.36	0.40	1

Trend Component	HP (100)	BK	CF	Hamilton
HP (100)	1			
BK	0.99	1		
CF	0.99	0.99	1	
Hamilton	0.94	0.93	0.92	1

BK = Baxter–King, CF = Christiano–Fitzgerald, HP = Hodrick–Prescott.
Source: Author's computations.

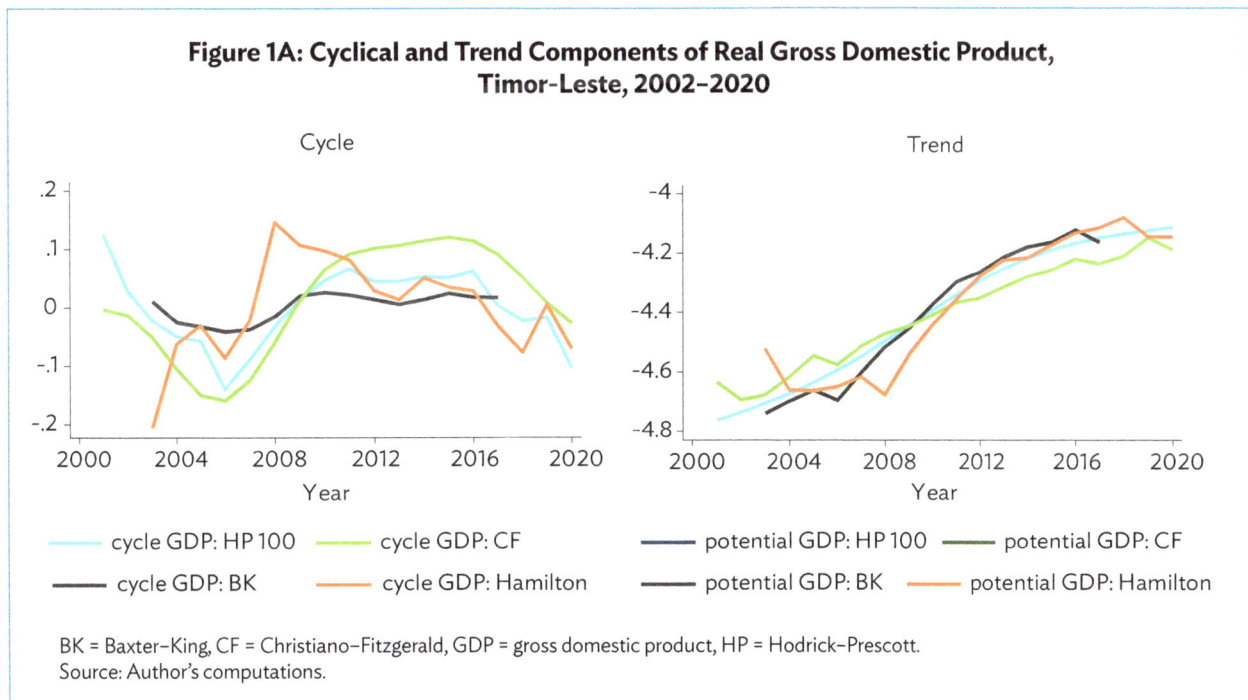

Figure 1A: Cyclical and Trend Components of Real Gross Domestic Product, Timor-Leste, 2002–2020

BK = Baxter–King, CF = Christiano–Fitzgerald, GDP = gross domestic product, HP = Hodrick–Prescott.
Source: Author's computations.

Empirical studies recognize the difficulties in providing accurate estimates of fiscal stabilizers but they also acknowledge the need to have at least approximations of it.[1] In what follows, we focus on a sample of 29 emerging and developing Asian countries with a special look at the Maldivian case using data between 1980 and 2020.[2]

Quantifying the stabilizing effect of fiscal policy requires assessing how fiscal policy affects economic activity. In a static setting, the empirical approach to measure the contribution "on impact" of fiscal policy to aggregate stability involves the estimation of the response of the relevant fiscal aggregate to changes in output.[3] The overall stabilizing role of fiscal policy is conceptually equivalent to the estimated sensitivity (or cyclicality) of a broad indicator of fiscal policy.[4] One good candidate variable is the budget balance (BB) (expressed as a percentage of gross domestic product [GDP]) which is an appropriate proxy for the aggregate demand's effect of fiscal policy in a given year.[5] That is,

$$BB = \alpha + \beta^{BB} \cdot growth + \varepsilon, \tag{B1}$$

where growth is the real GDP growth rate and β^{BB} captures the degree of overall fiscal stabilization (FISCO).[6] ε is a white noise disturbance satisfying usual assumptions.

When evaluating the stabilizing role of fiscal policy, a natural question is how much of the overall fiscal stabilization comes from the structural part of the budget and how much comes from automatic changes that are the result of the tax code and spending laws. In practice, answering this question requires decomposing the budget balance into a structural (cyclically adjusted) part and into an automatic part, and, consequently, assessing how these two components react to changes in economic activity.[7] The average stabilizing contribution of nonautomatic or "discretionary" fiscal actions can be identified by the sensitivity of the cyclically-adjusted balance (CAB) (expressed as a percentage of GDP). Moreover, the difference between the overall sensitivity and that stemming from the CAB can be attributed to automatic stabilizers. In mathematical form:

$$CAB = \alpha + \beta^{CAB} \cdot growth + \varepsilon, \tag{B2}$$

1   J. Cotis B. Crépon, Y. L'Horty, and R. Méary .1997. Les Stabilisateurs Automatiques sont-ils encore efficaces? Le cas de la France dans les années Quatre-Vingt-Dix; *Revue d'Economie Financière*, no 45. pp. 95-118. | A. Auerbach. 2002. Is There a Role Discretionary Fiscal Policy? NBER Working Paper Series. Working Paper No. 9306. National Bureau of Economic Research. November. https://www.nber.org/system/files/working_papers/w9306/w9306.pdf.

2   The sources of data are IMF's International Financial Statistics and IMF's World Economic Outlook (WEO).

3   P. R. Lane. 2003. The cyclical behaviour of fiscal policy: Evidence from the OECD. *Journal of Public Economics*. 87 (12). pp. 2661–2675. ScienceDirect, Elsevier. December. https://doi.org/10.1016/S0047-2727(02)00075-0. | A. Fatás and I. Mihov. 2012. Fiscal Policy as a Stabilization Tool. B.E. *Journal of Macroeconomics*. 12 (3). pp. 1-68. Walter de Gruyter GmbH. January. https://doi.org/10.1515/1935-1690.113.

4   On the one hand, the more countercyclical government spending is, the higher the fiscal stabilization. On the other, the more progressive the taxes are, the higher the fiscal stabilization.

5   In practice, the effectiveness of fiscal policy on aggregate demand and its effect in dampening volatility depends not only on how much fiscal policy reacts to changes in economic activity, but also on the size of fiscal multipliers. | O. J. Blanchard. 1993. Suggestions for a New Set of Fiscal Indicators. In H. A. A. Verbon and F. van Winden eds. *The Political Economy of Government Debt*. Amsterdam: Elsevier Science.

6   Assessing the sensitivity of counter-cyclical coefficients to different types of shocks is hindered by the difficulty in identifying the nature of such shocks and any formal analysis of the issue is bound to be tentative. We simply capture the sensitivity of the fiscal balance to changes in real GDP to capture both demand and supply disturbances.

7   When looking at the cyclical properties of the budget balance, it is common to split it into the cyclical balance and the cyclically-adjusted balance. | J. Galí and R. Perotti. 2003. Fiscal policy and monetary integration in Europe, *Economic Policy*. 18 (37). pp. 533–572. Oxford University Press. 1 October. https://doi.org/10.1111/1468-0327.00115_1. Changes in the cyclical balance give an estimate of the budgetary impact of aggregate fluctuations through the induced changes in tax bases and certain mandatory outlays. Subtracting the cyclical balance from the overall balance yields the cyclically-adjusted balance.

$$\beta^{AS} = \beta^{BB} - \beta^{CAB} \tag{B3}$$

where β^{CAB}, β^{AS} captures the degree of the stabilization attributable to "discretionary" fiscal actions and that attributable to the action of automatic stabilizers, respectively. ε is a white noise disturbance satisfying usual assumptions of zero mean and constant variance.

Table 2A shows the OLS results of β^{BB}, β^{CAB}, β^{AS} for each country and the entire time span (1990–2020) using as main regressor either real GDP growth or the output gap. Let's focus on columns 2–4. For Timor-Leste, fiscal policy in this period seems to have been acyclical in line with the majority of the other 27 countries out of 37 in the sample, hence not stabilizing (coefficient estimates are not statistically significant at the 10% level or higher). In Timor-Leste, this lack of a stabilizing role of fiscal policy comes from both the discretionary and automatic components. For most fragile and conflict-affected situations (FCAS), automatic stabilizers seem not to play a big role (some exceptions include Central African Republic, Côte d'Ivorie, Madagascar, Tuvalu, etc.). Regrettably, the discretionary component has been pro-cyclical in most countries for which one has a significant (negative) coefficient in column 3.

Table 2A: Fiscal Stabilization Estimation in Fragile and Conflict-Affected Situations, including Timor-Leste

Regressor	GDP Growth		
Sample / Dependent Variable	Overall Balance	Cyclically Adjusted Balance	Automatic Stabilizers
1	2	3	4
Timor-Leste	−0.698	−1.314	0.616
Afghanistan	−0.019	0.059	−0,078
Angola	0.560**	–	–
Bosnia and Herzegovina	0.182	−0.018	0.200
Burundi	0.123	0.215	−0.092
Central African Republic	0.097	−0.129*	0.227***
Chad	−0.073	0.135	−0.208
Comoros	0.151	0.084	0.067
Democratic Republic of Congo	0.108*	–	–
Republic of Congo	0.816*	0.451	0.365
Côte d'Ivorie	−0.097*	−0.239***	0.142**
Eritrea	0.441	0.317	0.124
Guinea	0.371**	0.197	0.174
Guinea-Bissau	0.106	−0.108	0.214**
Haiti	−0.100	−0.688**	0.588*
Iraq	−0.790***	−0.264	−0.526*
Kiribati	2.840**	1.467	1.373
Kosovo	0.566*	0.568*	−0.002

| Regressor | | GDP Growth | |
| Sample / Dependent Variable | Overall Balance | Cyclically Adjusted Balance | Automatic Stabilizers |
1	2	3	4
Liberia	−0.007	−0.042	0.035
Libya	0.346	−0.102	0.448**
Madagascar	0.233***	0.069	0.164*
Malawi	0.403	1.119	−0.716
Mali	−0.048	−0.083	0.035
Marshall Islands	−0.221	−0.476	0.255
Federated States of Micronesia	−0.005	−0.549	0.545
Myanmar	−0.100	−0.489	0.390
Nepal	−0.388	−0.638	0.250
Sierra Leone	0.021	−0.069	0.091
Solomon Islands	0.181	−0.124	0.306
South Sudan	0.125	1.726	−1.600
Sudan	0.188	2.800	−2.612
Syria	−0.320**	−0.451***	0.131
Sao Tome and Principe	−1.209	2.537	−3.746
Togo	0.072	−0.151*	0.223***
Tuvalu	1.224	0.628	0.596
Yemen	0.091	−0.056	0.147
Zimbabwe	0.087	0.440	−0.353

Notes:
1. Robust standard errors not shown for reasons of parsimony.
2. A constant term was included but omitted for reasons of parsimony.
3. * denotes statistical significance at the 10% level.
4. ** denotes statistical significance at the 5% level.
5. *** denotes statistical significance at the 1% level.
Source: Author's computations.

To test the stability of these results over time, equation (B1) was generalized by introducing the assumption that the regression coefficients may vary over time:

$$1. \quad BB = \alpha_t + \beta_t^{BB} \cdot growth + \varepsilon, \qquad\qquad (B4)$$

We use a rolling regression method with a length of 10 years. Figure 2A shows the interquartile range for the sample of FCAS listed in Table 1 for the case of the overall fiscal stabilization. It seems that over time, the overall stabilization role of fiscal policy has been relatively stable and mostly acyclical throughout the period. Panel b plots the Timorese case where one can observe that the initially pro-cyclical nature of fiscal policy (between 2010 and 2015) just got weaker and moved toward acyclical over time.

Figure 2A: Interquartile Time Evolution of Time-Varying Coefficients of Overall Fiscal Stabilization in Fragile and Conflict-Affected Situations versus Timor-Leste

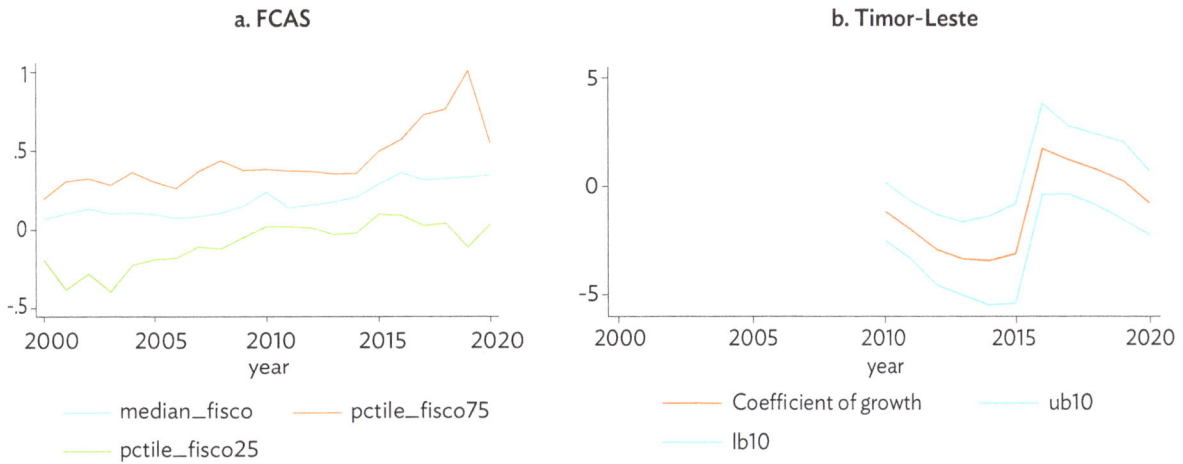

a. FCAS

b. Timor-Leste

median_fisco   pctile_fisco75

pctile_fisco25

Coefficient of growth   ub10

lb10

FISCO = overall fiscal stabilization, FCAS = fragile and conflict-affected situation, pctile = percentile, ub=upper bound; lb=lower bound.
Note: Panel (a) interquartile range, bottom and top 25th percentiles (green and orange respectively) plus median (blue). Panel (b) time-varying FISCO in orange plus 90% confidence bands plotted in blue in the Timorese case.
Source: Author's computations.

APPENDIX 3
TAX CAPACITY IN ASIA

The stochastic frontier model of Aigner et al. (1977) is the standard econometric method for tax capacity estimates.[1] The current analysis is most related to Langford and Ohlenburg (2016)[2] and Committeri and Pessino (2013)[3] who likewise carried out stochastic frontier analyses based on panel data to provide cross country estimates of tax potential and effort. However, the present study differs significantly in terms of the number of countries included, the data used, and time period under focus. A panel version of this model can be written as:

$$\ln\tau_{it} = \alpha + \beta^{\pi}x_{it} + v_{it} - u_{it} \tag{C1}$$

where u_{it} represents the inefficiency, a non-negative random variable associated with country-specific factors which contribute to country i not attaining its tax capacity at time t. $u_{it} > 0$. τ_{it} represents the tax revenue to gross domestic product (GDP) ratio for country i at time t. x_{it} is a vector that represents independent variables affecting tax revenue for country i at time t; β^{π} is a vector of unknown parameters. v_{it} is the residual, a random stochastic variable. We assume that v_{it} has a symmetric distribution, such as the normal distribution, and v_{it} and u_{it} are statistically independent of each other.[4] We then define tax effort (a value between zero and one) as:

$$TE_{it} = \frac{\tau_{it}}{\exp(\alpha+\beta^{T}x_{it} + v_{it})} = \frac{\exp(\alpha+\beta^{T}x_{it} + v_{it} - u_{it})}{\exp(\alpha+\beta^{T}x_{it} + v_{it})} = \exp(-u_{it}) \tag{C2}$$

We compute country-specific estimates of tax effort and tax capacity using a panel dataset of 103 countries from 1990 to 2018 drawing upon data from the IMF's World Economic Outlook and the World Bank's World Development Indicators databases. To allow more generality into the stochastic frontier model, while guarding against distribution misspecification, a variety of one-sided distributions have been proposed for modeling u_{it}. Stevenson (1980) proposed the truncated-normal distribution as a generalization of the half-normal distribution; whereas the half-normal distribution is the truncation of the $N(0, \sigma_u^2)$ at 0, the truncated-normal distribution is the truncation of the $N(\mu, \sigma_u^2)$ at 0. The pre-truncation mean parameter, μ, affords the stochastic frontier model more flexibility in the shape of the distribution of inefficiency.[5]

Table 3A reports the model parameter estimates for all countries.[6] Under the two models, most coefficients and the lambda factor[7] are statistically significant at 1% level and have the expected signs (Table 3A). These findings are in line with those from Mawaejje and Sebudde (2019) (cf. Table 2 in their paper).[8] Consistent with previous studies,

---

1   D. Aigner, C. K. Lovell, and P. Schmidt. 1977. Formulation and estimation of stochastic frontier production function models. *Journal of Econometrics*. 6 (1). pp. 21–37. ScienceDirect, Elsevier. July. https://www.sciencedirect.com/science/article/abs/pii/0304407677900525.
2   B. Langford and T. Ohlenburg. 2016. Tax Revenue Potential and Effort: An Empirical Investigation. *Working Paper S-43202-UGA-1*. International Growth Centre, London School of Economics and Political Science. London.
3   M. Committeri and C. Pessino. 2013. Understanding Countries' Tax Effort. *IMF Working Papers*. No. 2013/244, Washington, DC: International Monetary Fund. 16 December. https://www.imf.org/en/Publications/WP/Issues/2016/12/31/Understanding-Countries-Tax-Effort-41132.
4   Note that the inefficiency effects u_{it} as well as the symmetric error terms v_{it} may carry the effects of measurement errors in the dependent variables, just as in any other econometric model.
5   The normal-half normal model of Aigner et al. (1977) can be obtained through maximum likelihood estimates. | Footnote 1 of Appendix 3.
6   Cross-section estimation techniques, whether in the context of the peer analysis or of stochastic frontier analysis, cannot fully capture the effects of country-specific circumstances and may bias estimates of the revenue gaps or tax effort. Given these and other data imitations, results should be interpreted with caution.
7   *Lambda* (σui /σvi) provides information of the relative contribution of v_{it} and u_{it} to the total error term.
8   Note, however, that the tax effort, tax capacity and tax potential figures obtained in Table 4 are not comparable with those in this note. While Mawaejje and Sebudde (2019) used a sample of 150 countries to apply the stochastic frontier method, here a much smaller sample comprising solely of Asian economies was used. There are also differences in the time period covered by the two studies. It is worth noting

countries with a higher level of public expenditure on education and per capita GDP are near their tax capacity.[9] Also, in line with prior evidence, the size of the agricultural sector and the Gini coefficient are also highly significant variables with an inverse relationship with tax capacity and tax effort.[10] All coefficients are statistically significant (different from zero) at the 5% level and have the expected signs. Moreover, in both models the coefficients are quite similar; they include the same explanatory variables. The lambda parameter, λi ($\sigma ui / \sigma vi$), is quite large (greater than 2.8) and statistically significant.

Table 3A: Parameter Estimates of the Stochastic Frontier Tax Function—All Countries

Variable	Half Normal		Truncated Normal	
	Coefficient	Standard error	Coefficient	Standard error
Constant	-6.125***	0.714		
Real gross domestic product per capita	1.931***	0.150	1.941***	0.144
Real gross domestic product per capita square	-0.972***	0.0079	-0.979***	0.0075
Agriculture share in total value added	-0.011***	0.0013	-0.113***	0.0013
Public expenditure in education	0.041***	0.003	0.041***	0.0032
Trade openness	0.0005****	0.00014	0.00057***	0.00014
Gini index	-0.170***	0.053	-0.181***	0.054
Inefficiency				
Lambda 1/	6.935***	0.045	3.167***	0.270
Sigma (σ) 1/	0.597***	0.045	0.175***	0.047

Notes:
1. * denotes statistical significance at the 10% level.
2. ** denotes statistical significance at the 5% level.
3. *** denotes statistical significance at the 1% level.
4. 1/ parameters for compound error.
5. The parameter lambda (λ) indicates the share of technical inefficiency in the total error variance, and the parameter Sigma (σ), which is similarly reparameterized, indicates the share of total variance accounted for by inefficiency.

Source: Author's computations.

  that Mawaejje and Sebudde (2019) include several advanced economies, which influences the determination of the frontier against which all sample countries are compared against. In our study, given that there are only Asian countries, the resulting benchmarks for tax effort, tax capacity and tax potential are different. | J. Mawejje and R. Sebudde. 2019. Tax revenue potential and effort: Worldwide estimates using a new dataset. *Economic Analysis and Policy*. 63. pp. 119–129. ScienceDirect, Elsevier. https://doi.org/10.1016/j.eap.2019.05.005.

9 V. Tanzi. 1987. Quantitative Characteristics of the Tax Systems of Developing Countries, in David Newbery and Nicholas Stern (eds). 1987. *The Theory of Taxation in Developing Countries*. Oxford University Press. | J. R. Lotz and E. R. Morss. 1967. Measuring 'Tax Effort' in Developing Countries. IMF Staff Papers. 14 (3). pp. 478–499. International Monetary Fund. January. https://www.elibrary.imf.org/view/journals/024/1967/003/article-A004-en.xml.

10 V. Tanzi and H. R. Davoodi. 1997. Corruption, Public Investment and Growth. *IMF Working Papers*. No. 1997/139. Washington, DC: International Monetary Fund. October. https://www.imf.org/en/Publications/WP/Issues/2016/12/30/Corruption-Public-Investment-and-Growth-2353. | D. A. Grigorian and H. R. Davoodi. 2007. Tax Potential vs. Tax Effort: A Cross-Country Analysis of Armenia's Stubbornly Low Tax Collection. *IMF Working Papers*. No. 2007/106. Washington, DC: International Monetary Fund. May. https://www.imf.org/en/Publications/WP/Issues/2016/12/31/Tax-Potential-vs-20642. | Footnote 9 of Appendix 3 (2nd citation).

APPENDIX 4
TAX BUOYANCY IN FRAGILE AND CONFLICT-AFFECTED SITUATIONS: A VIEW OF TIMOR-LESTE'S CASE

The buoyancy of a tax system measures the total response of tax revenue both to changes in national income and to discretionary changes in tax policies over time (such as the ones discussed in chapter 3), and it is traditionally interpreted as the percentage change in revenue associated to a 1% change in income. Let T be total tax revenue, and Y be gross domestic product (GDP), buoyancy is measured as:

$$b_{T,Y} = \frac{\partial T}{\partial Y} * \frac{Y}{T} \qquad \text{(D1)}$$

Though closely related to buoyancy, the elasticity of the tax system measures instead the responsiveness of tax revenue to changes in national income keeping all other parameters (including tax legislation) constant.[1] When the elasticity of major revenue sources is low (for example, owing to the rigidity of the tax base or the presence of tax evasion or avoidance), governments raise additional resources through discretionary measures. In this case, the growth of tax revenue comes through high buoyancy rather than high elasticity.[2]

Empirically, the buoyancy (or elasticity) of a tax can be obtained by a linear regression:

$$T = \alpha + \beta Y + \varepsilon \qquad \text{(D2)}$$

where α is a constant, β is the marginal rate of taxation, ε is an error term. Since $\partial T / \partial Y = \beta$, it follows that buoyancy (or elasticity) $B_{T,Y} = \beta(Y/T)$. This method involves the estimation of β and calculation of the term (Y/T) by averaging Y and T over the sample period in order to eliminate cyclical influences. An alternative method, which is followed in this study, is to express equation (D2) in exponential form:

$$T = \alpha Y^{\beta} \varepsilon \qquad \text{(D3)}$$

Based on equation (D3), revenue buoyancy and elasticity are traditionally estimated by means of a regression of the logarithm of tax revenue (or a subcomponent) on the logarithm of GDP. This is the approach followed here.

$$\log T = \log \alpha + \beta \log Y + \varepsilon \qquad \text{(D4)}$$

Two issues emerge when estimating tax buoyancy and elasticity. The first relates to the time span over which the response of revenues to GDP is considered. Over the long run, it is generally expected that buoyancy is equal to 1. If not, at least on theoretical grounds, there would come a point when revenues exceed 100% of their respective bases. However, in the short run, buoyancies can be different from 1 and they can be different across revenue items.[3] A second

---

1   R. Skeete, K. Coppin, and D. Boamah. 2003. Elasticities and Buoyancies of the Barbados Tax System, 1977–1999. *Working Papers*. Central Bank of Barbados. July. http://www.centralbank.org.bb/Portals/0/Files/WP2003-12.pdf.

2   In some sense, elasticity is more appropriately used to estimate the impact on revenues from, say, an unexpected decline in the tax base (owing, for example, to a disaster triggered by natural hazard), or the increase in, say, personal income tax revenues over time if other provisions (income brackets, deductions, and allowances) remain the same. Buoyancy on the other hand, more appropriately measures past revenue developments or the combined effects of a package of reforms.

3   For example, in the short-run the PIT may increase more than proportionally to income if the revenue brackets, or deductions, are not

issue relates to the time series properties of revenue and income, specifically the amount of inertia that each has and whether there exists a stable long-run relationship between them. In general, both the logarithm of tax revenue (or a component) and the logarithm of GDP are integrated, and it is reasonable to expect that they are co-integrated. With these considerations in mind, the analysis is based on the unrestricted error correction autoregressive distributed lag (ARDL) (p,q) representation on a sample of 37 fragile and conflict-affected situations (FCAS) between 1990–2019:[4]

$$\Delta \ln y_{it} = \varphi_i y_{it-1} + \beta'_i x_{it-1} + \sum_{j=1}^{p-1} \lambda_{ij} \Delta \ln y_{it-j} + \sum_{q=1}^{q-1} \gamma'_{ij} \Delta \ln x_{it-j} + \mu_i + \xi_{it}, i = 1, 2, ..., N; t = 1, 2, ..., T \quad \text{(D5)}$$

where y_{it} is the natural logarithm of a scalar dependent tax revenue variable, x_{it} is the k x 1 vector of regressors for group I (which includes the natural logarithm of GDP but also other potential controls), μ_i represents the fixed effects, φ_i is a scalar coefficient on the lagged dependent variable. β'_i is the k x 1 vector of coefficients on explanatory variables, λ_{ij}'s are scalar coefficients on lagged first-differences of dependent variables, and γ_{ij}'s are k x 1 coefficient vectors on first-differences of explanatory variables and their lagged values.[5] Assuming that $\varphi_i < 0$ for all i, there exists a long-run relationship between y_{it} and x_{it} defined as:

$$\ln y_{it} = \theta'_i \ln x_{it} + \eta_{i-t}, i = 1, 2, ..., N; t = 1, 2, ..., T \quad \text{(D6)}$$

where $\theta'_i = -\beta'_i / \varphi_i$ is the k x 1 vector of the long-run coefficients, and η_{it}'s are stationary with possible non-zero means. Equation (D5) can then be rewritten as:

$$\Delta \ln y_{it} = \varphi_i \eta_{it-1} + \sum_{j=1}^{p-1} \lambda_{ij} \Delta \ln y_{it-j} + \sum_{q=1}^{q-1} \gamma'_{ij} \Delta \ln x_{it-j} + \mu_i + \xi_{it}, i = 1, 2, ..., N; t = 1, 2, ..., T \quad \text{(D7)}$$

where η_{it-1} is the error correction term, and φ_i measures the speed of adjustment toward the long-run equilibrium.

We estimate equation (D7) in a panel setting. Note that the logarithm of the tax revenue (and its components) and the logarithm of GDP are non-stationary and co-integrated. Exploiting the panel dimension has several advantages.[6] In terms of estimators, we consider the Mean Group estimator which is appropriate for the analysis of dynamic panels with both large time and cross-section dimensions,[7] and they have the advantage of accommodating both the long-run equilibrium and the possibly heterogeneous dynamic adjustment process.[8] In what follows, we test the null hypothesis that the long-run coefficient is equal to one, and, in case of rejection, we test whether it is greater or smaller than one.

---

adjusted for inflation. Similarly, owing to provisions such as loss-carry forward, CIT collection might increase less than VAT collection during the economic rebound that follows a recession.

4   Macroeconomic and fiscal data retrieved from the IMF's International Financial Statistics and Government Financial Statistics.

5   We assume that the disturbances ξ_{it} in the ARDL model are independently distributed across i and t, with zero means and constant variances. Equation (D5) implies that developments in tax revenues can be explained by a distributed lag of order p of the dependent variable, and a distributed lag of order q of GDP.

6   First, it enables bypassing lack of degree-of-freedom related to (potentially) short spanned time series at the cross-section level. Second, hypothesis testing is more powerful and inference stronger than when using time series techniques on only one country. Third, cross-sectional information reduces the probability of a spurious regression. | A. Banerjee. 2002. Panel Data Unit Roots and Cointegration: An Overview. *Oxford Bulletin of Economic and Statistics.* 61 (S1). pp. 607–630. Wiley Online Library. 10 December. https://onlinelibrary.wiley.com/doi/epdf/10.1111/1468-0084.0610s1607.

7   M. H. Pesaran and R. Smith. 1995. Estimating long-run relationship from dynamic heterogeneous panels. *Journal of Econometrics*, 68 (1). pp. 79–113. ScienceDirect, Elsevier. July. https://doi.org/10.1016/0304-4076(94)01644-F.

8   These estimators allow correcting for the potential bias that could result from estimating tax buoyancy coefficients using standard fixed-effects models in the presence of nonstationary error terms, which imposing parameter homogeneity would introduce into the estimating equation.

We also try to understand variations in the stabilization role of taxation during periods of economic expansion and economic contraction. To empirically explore whether tax buoyancy varies depending on the phase of the business cycle, the following alternative short-run non-linear regression is estimated:

$$\Delta \ln y_{it} = \alpha_i^k + \beta_k^{recession} \cdot Y(z) \cdot \Delta \ln x_{it} + \beta_k^{expansion} \cdot (1 - Y(z)) \cdot \Delta \ln x_{it} + \mu_i + \eta_t + \varepsilon_{i,t}^k \qquad \text{(D8)}$$

$$\text{with } Y(z_{it}) = \frac{\exp(-\gamma z_{it})}{1 + \exp(-\gamma z_{it})}, \gamma > 0$$

in which z_{it} is an indicator of the state of the economy normalized to have zero mean and unit variance. The weights assigned to each regime vary between 0 and 1 according to the weighting function $F(.)$, so that $F(z_{it})$ can be interpreted as the probability of being in a given state of the economy.[9] We choose $\gamma = 1.5$,[10] so that the economy spends about 20% of the time in a recessionary regime—defined as $F(z_{it}) > 0.8$.[11] This is equivalent to the smooth transition autoregressive (STAR) model developed by Granger and Teräsvirta (1993) to inspect nonlinearities.[12] The question then is what to use as an indicator for the variable z_{it}. Commonly, real GDP growth is used as a proxy for the state of the economy. We use this as a baseline option and the Hodrick–Prescott based output gap as the second alternative.

To test the stability of these results over time, we generalize equation (D4) by introducing the assumption that the regression coefficients may vary over time. We use a rolling regression method with a length of 10 years. Figure 4A shows the interquartile range for the same sample of Asian economies for the case of the overall tax buoyancy. In general, buoyancy has been increasing over time and converging among the sample (as shown by the narrower top and bottom quartiles in the more recent period). Both indirect taxes and other taxes seem to have contributed to this increase over time while direct taxes have had a downward trend since 2015. Overall, this is good and promising news going forward.

---

9   The coefficients $\beta_k^{recession}$ and $\beta_k^{expansion}$ capture the buoyancy impact at each horizon k in cases of extreme recessions ($F(z_{it}) \approx 1$ when z goes to minus infinity) and booms ($1 - F(z_{it}) \approx 1$ when z goes to plus infinity), respectively. $F(z_{it}) = 0.5$ is the cutoff between weak and strong economic activity.

10 Following A. Auerbach and Y. Gorodnichenko. 2012. Measuring the Output Responses to Fiscal Policy. *American Economic Journal: Economic Policy.* 4 (2). pp. 1–27. American Economic Association. May. https://pubs.aeaweb.org/doi/pdfplus/10.1257/pol.4.2.1.

11 Our results hardly change when using alternative values of the parameter γ between 1 and 6.

12 Compared with a model in which each dependent variable would be interacted with a measure of the business cycle position, an advantage of this approach is the fact that it permits a direct test of whether the tax buoyancy varies in recessions and expansions. By having the F(.) varying across a continuum of states, this makes the state-contingent buoyancy change smoothly making the estimations in each state more stable and precise. See T. Singh. 2012. Testing nonlinearities in economic growth in the OECD Countries: An evidence from SETAR and STAR models. *Applied Economics.* 44 (30). pp. 3887–3908. Routledge. June. https://doi.org/10.1080/00036846.2011.583221. | T. Singh. 2014. On the regime-switching and asymmetric dynamics of economic growth in the OECD Countries. *Research in Economics.* 68 (2). pp. 169–192. ScienceDirect, Elsevier. June. https://doi.org/10.1016/j.rie.2013.12.004 and A.C. Silva Lopes and G.F. Zsurkis. 2019. Are linear models really unuseful to describe business cycle data? *Applied Economics.* 51 (22). pp. 2355–2376. Routledge. July. https://doi.org/10.1080/00036846.2018.1495825 for a review and discussion of nonlinear models.

Figure 4A: Interquartile Time Evolution of Buoyancy Time-Varying Coefficients, Asia

Overall Buoyancy

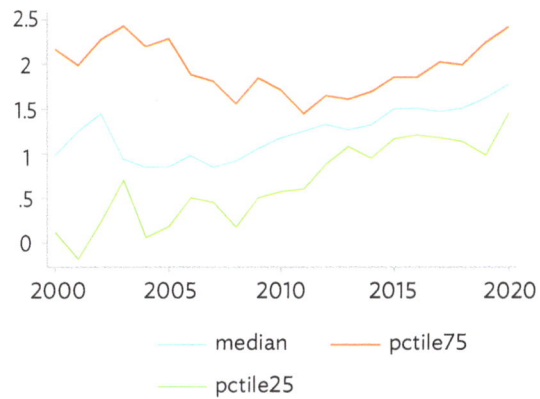

Indirect Taxes

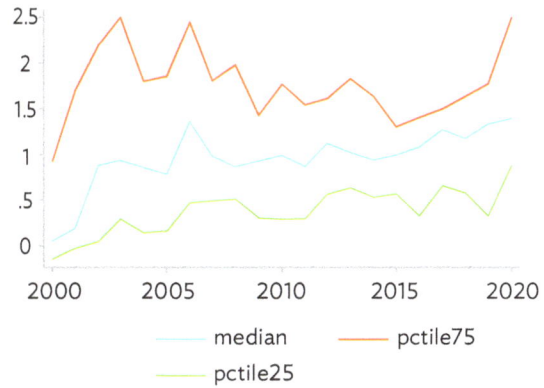

Direct Taxes

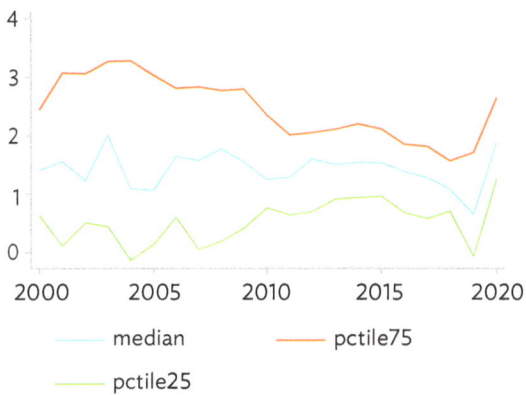

Other Taxes

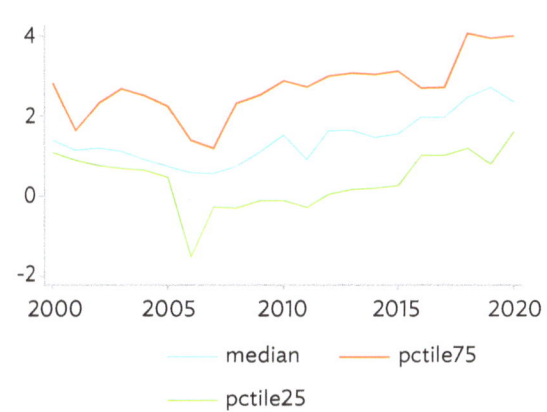

pctile = percentile.
Source: Author's computations.

APPENDIX 5
MACROECONOMIC EFFECT OF STRUCTURAL REFORMS IN FRAGILE AND CONFLICT-AFFECTED SITUATIONS

The specification of the key local projection method regression takes the following form:[1]

$$y_{t+k,i} - y_{t-1,i} = \alpha_i + \gamma_t + \beta_k R_{i,t} + \theta X_{i,t} + \varepsilon_{i,t} \tag{E1}$$

in which y is the log of a key macroeconomic variable (log of real gross domestic product, log of employment, log of labor productivity); t and i are the time and country dimensions, respectively; k = 0, 1, 2,...; α_i denotes country fixed effects, included to control for unobserved cross-country heterogeneity; γ_t denotes time fixed effects, included to take account of global factors such as shifts in oil prices or the global business cycle; $R_{i,t}$ denotes the structural reform; X is a set of control variables including past economic growth and past reforms; and $\varepsilon_{i,t}$ is an independent and identically distributed disturbance term satisfying standard assumptions of zero mean and constant variance.

Equation (E1) is estimated for each k=0,..,6. Impulse response functions are computed using the estimated coefficients β_k, and the confidence bands associated with the estimated impulse-response functions are obtained using the estimated standard errors of the coefficients β_k, based on robust standard errors clustered at the country level. The macroeconomic series used in the analysis come from a database that covers an unbalanced sample of advanced, emerging, and low-income countries over the 1970–2014 period.[2] Econometrically, estimating equation (E1) for a sample of fragile and conflicted-affected situations yields the impulse response functions (IRFs) depicted in Figure 13 in the main text.

---

1   O. Jordà. 2005. Estimation and Inference of Impulse Responses by Local Projections. *American Economic Review*. 95 (1). pp. 161 -182. https://www.aeaweb.org/articles?id=10.1257/0002828053828518.
2   Footnote 100 of Chapter 5.

To estimate the dynamic response of income distribution proxies to tax revenue reforms, we follow the local projection method proposed by Jordà (2005) to estimate impulse–response functions.[1] Income inequality proxies, namely the Gini index, are obtained from the Standardized World Income Inequality Database, constructed by Solt (2009).[2] To identify the episodes of large tax revenue mobilization, we rely on a dataset put together by Akitoby et al. (2019) who focused on countries with more tangible tax revenue mobilization results:[3] (i) countries that have increased their tax-to-gross domestic product (GDP) ratios by a minimum of 0.5% each year for at least 3 consecutive years (or 1.5% within 3 years); (ii) countries with beyond average increases in their tax-to-GDP ratios; and/or (iii) countries with better tax performance compared with peers in the same income group. Reforms include any changes that correspond to a new tax policy, changes in tax rates, changes in the tax base, and changes in exemptions; in sum, all changes that are revenue enhancing (see Akitoby et al. [2019] for further details). Akitoby et al. (2019) include tax reforms for 45 countries between 2000 and 2015 of which 8 are from Asia.[4]

The baseline specification is:

$$y_{t+k,i} - y_{t-1,i} = \alpha_i + \beta_k R_{i,t} + \theta X_{i,t} + \varepsilon_{i,t} \qquad \text{(F1)}$$

in which i denotes the cross-sectional unit, i.e., number of countries, and t denotes the time in years; y is the dependent variable of interest, namely, an income distribution proxy; β_k denotes the (cumulative) response of the variable of interest in each k year after the tax revenue reform; α_i are country fixed effects; $R_{i,t}$ denotes the tax revenue reform shock defined in binary terms in the area considered for country i at year t.[5] If there are sequences of years with the same type of reform, we focus only on the first year of a given tax reform episode to improve the identification and minimize reverse causality problems. All revenue mobilization reform shocks featured in our analysis are country-wide shocks. $X_{i,t}$ is a set a of control variables including two lags of tax reform shocks, two lags of real GDP growth, and two lags of the dependent variable.[6] Equation (F1) is estimated using ordinary least squares (OLS). The impulse response functions (IRFs) are then obtained by plotting the estimated β_k for k= 0,1,..5 confidence bands computed using the standard deviations associated with the estimated coefficients β_k—based on robust standard errors clustered at the country level.[7]

1   Footnote 1 of Appendix 5. | The local projection method has been advocated by Auerbach and Gorodnichenko (2013) as a flexible alternative to vector autoregression (or autoregressive distributed lag) specifications. | Footnote 10 of Appendix 4.
2   F. Solt. 2009. Standardizing the World Income Inequality Database. *Social Science Quarterly*. 90 (2). pp. 231–242. Wiley-Blackwell. April. https://doi.org/10.1111/j.1540-6237.2009.00614.x.
3   B. Akitoby et al. 2019. Tax revenue mobilization episodes in developing countries. *Policy Design and Practice*. 3 (2). pp. 1–29. Informa UK (Taylor & Francis). November. https://doi.org/10.1080/25741292.2019.1685729.
4   Cambodia, the Lao PDR, Maldives, Nepal, Philippines, Solomon Islands, Tonga, Tuvalu.
5   Reforms are country specific and not weighted. Akitoby et al. (2019) do not provide narrative information on every reform, so each of them is treated equally for econometric purposes. | Footnote 3 of Appendix 6.
6   While the Nickel-bias may be a problem, papers such as Acemoglu et al. (2019) have argued that T as small as 40 should make the bias in panel LPM estimators relatively small. | D. Acemoglu et al. 2019. Democracy Does Cause Growth. *Journal of Political Economy*.127 (1). pp. 47–100. The University of Chicago Press. February. https://doi.org/10.1086/700936. | In our case, the finite sample bias is in the order of 1/T, where T in our sample is 16. That said, similar results are obtained when we applied the bias-corrected alternative (LSDVC) via the method proposed by Bruno (2005) (the Arellano–Bond consistent estimator was used to initialize the bias correction). | G. Bruno. 2005. Estimation and Inference in Dynamic Unbalanced Panel-data Models with a Small Number of Individuals. *The Stata Journal*. 5 (4). pp. 473–500. SAGE Publishing. December. https://doi.org/10.1177/1536867X0500500401.
7   Another advantage of the local projection method compared to vector autoregression (autoregressive distributed lag) specifications is that the computation of confidence bands does not require Monte Carlo simulations or asymptotic approximations. One limitation, however, is that confidence bands at longer horizons tend to be wider than those estimated in vector autoregression specifications.

ADDITIONAL REFERENCES FOR TECHNICAL APPENDIXES

1. C.W.J. Granger and Timo Teräsvirta. 1993. *Modelling Nonlinear Economic Relationships*. Oxford University Press.
2. R.J. Hodrick. 2020. An Exploration of Trend-Cycle Decomposition Methodologies in Simulated Data. NBER Working paper Series. Working Paper No. 26750. National Bureau of Economic Research. https://www.nber.org/system/files/working_papers/w26750/w26750.pdf.
3. V. Tanzi. 1968. Comparing International Tax 'Burdens': A Suggested Method. *Journal of Political Economy*. 76 (5). pp. 1078–1084. The University of Chicago Press. September–October. https://doi.org/10.1086/259470.